THE ELEGANCE WITH EASE COOKBOOK

THE ELEGANCE WITH EASE COOKBOOK

Fern Lebo

INCORPORATED
MAPLEWOOD, NEW JERSEY   07040

Library of Congress Cataloging in Publication Data

Lebo, Fern.
  The elegance with ease cookbook.

  1. Cookery.   I. Title.
TX715.L445   641.5   80-11183
ISBN 0-8437-3347-0

Printed in Canada

Cover Photo:
Shrimp Stroganoff, page 63

THE ELEGANCE WITH EASE COOKBOOK

To the men in my life

CONTENTS

SOUPS

SALAD SAMPLERS

SIDE DISHES AND SNICKLESNACKLES

INTRODUCTION

The Elegance with Ease Cookbook is a practical guide carefully designed for everyone *but* the true gourmet cook. It has been written for people who like to eat and entertain well, even lavishly, but don't want to spend a lifetime in preparation. It is dedicated to the short cutter, the time saver, and the addicted can opener.

There are other cookbooks on the market which promise easy recipes, and some of them actually succeed in keeping that promise — but at the cost of elegance. The easy ones, at best, look easy and, at worst, taste uneasy. The difference with the recipes in this book is that they look and taste as though they take hours and require a great deal of skill. In fact they don't, but it does take ingenuity to make their preparation wonderfully simple. And that's what makes them special.

This, then, is a book for the secretive cheater; for the person who would like to develop a happy reputation for being a terrific cook with a flair for entertaining easily.

The culinary secret to creative cheating in the kitchen is what I like to call "dump recipes." Even some semi-great chefs are privy to this secret (although they'd swallow their pepper grinders before admitting it). One simply opens a can, and dumps. The talent comes in selecting the right can to complement the creation. And having grown up in the shiny, stainless steel kitchens of restaurants and resorts, watching whitely starched gentlemen in cream puff hats make use of this skill, I would like to pass on the results to you — they are delectable.

Since many of the recipes are, in great measure, dependent on the cans and bottles you choose to open, select only those brands you know well and can truly count on for their consistent flavor and texture. Exact measurements aren't nearly as important to the creative cook as are dependable ingredients.

If "cuisine à la can" makes you feel a little uneasy, put your fears to rest. In *Nutrition For Good Health* (Plycon Press, 1974) Frederick J. Stare, M.D. and Margaret McWilliams, Ph.D. state: "So-called health foods, organically grown foods, and natural foods are no more necessary for good nutrition than the green cheese of the moon which our astronauts did not find. Every food when properly used is a health food… Every food is an organic food and a fertile soil is filled with hundreds of organic and inorganic substances necessary for its development and growth. Every food is a natural food or made from natural sources."

Learn to cheat — graciously, and while you're at it, remember the 11th Commandment…garnish lavishly. Parsley sprigs, carrot curls, radish rosettes and cherry tomatoes have a talent for making it look like you've spent endless hours creating in the kitchen.

For all of us great pretenders, here's a cookbook that guarantees elegant dining — with the greatest of ease!

A Word About Ingredients

Before you reach for your can-opener, just a few tips. When we call for a can of soup, we mean *condensed* soup — and no diluting it unless the recipe says so.

Canned fruits and vegetables should be drained unless the recipe says otherwise.

Canned shrimp, crab and lobster make gourmet cooking a bed of roses — but even roses have thorns, and these handy little cans often include the odd scrap of shell. So take half a minute to pick them over before you dump.

If you marinate meat for more than a couple of hours, it's safest to do so in the fridge. But remember to bring it to room temperature before cooking, or else add a little to the cooking time.

A Metric Note

Worried about a metric future? Hang onto this cookbook — I've included simple metric equivalents with every recipe. So, when a 10 oz. can of soup is transformed into a 300 mL can, you can still enjoy the tasty treats calling for that ingredient. Buy the metric size closest to the one listed.

And don't be afraid to remodel your kitchen! A new oven, with a temperature dial marked in degrees Celsius, bakes a great meat loaf.

Cooking, metric style, is even easier than the "old" way. Teaspoons, tablespoons, cups, pints, and fluid ounces will *all* be replaced by millilitres. You can forget the old "tables;" just measure and pour. (And if you've been confused by Canadian quarts, U.S. quarts, and U.K. quarts — forget them! A litre is a litre all over the world.)

The Appendix provides a table of Metric Units, and one of Standard Metric Kitchen Measures, as well as a Customary-to-Metric Conversion Chart.

Main Dishes

Pretty good meat loaf

Serves 4-6

Almost everyone who doesn't want to spend hours in the kitchen purchases, as part of the weekly shopping chore, some ground meat — because it looks fast. The problem then arises: what to do with it?

The easiest answer to this common kitchen conundrum is usually meat loaf. And every adequate cook has at least one questionable recipe in her collection for this old standby. Generally though, when she presents it to her family, she wishes she hadn't.

Here is a recipe that goes beyond the ordinary to achieve, at least, pretty good results. The whole thing should take only a minute or two to squish together, even for the most inexperienced hands. And while you have to recognize that you're not creating a dazzler, you are putting together a satisfying dish.

For that added touch, garnish with parsley sprigs (which, when lightly washed, shaken and stuffed into a plastic bag, last for weeks in the vegetable cooler of your refrigerator) and neatly sliced circles of hard-boiled egg.

If you want to make it taste better yet, dress your table and serve with wine. Makes it look like you went all out.

Ingredients

2 lbs. (1 kg) ground beef
1 packet dehydrated onion soup
1/4 cup (50 mL) bread crumbs or wheat germ
1 egg
1/4 cup (50 mL) ketchup or chili sauce

Method

Combine all the ingredients but reserve the ketchup or chili sauce to pour on top for the last 10 minutes of baking. Shape into a loaf and bake in a greased (non-stick sprays are super for this) loaf pan at 350°F (180°C) for about 1 hour.

You may make individual loaves by dividing into greased muffin tins which you then bake for half the usual time.

Serve with a starch (like mashed potatoes…the instant kind, using milk instead of water and a generous dollop of butter) plus a vegetable or two.

Muddle meat loaf

Serves 4-6

If it's all the same to you, I'd like to introduce you to another successful meat loaf recipe because, like the scenery, a change is as good as a rest.

This marvelous little dump recipe made its debut in my friend Connie's kitchen. Connie is one of those wonderfully organized women whose dialing finger has been cleverly trained to recall the numbers of all the best catering establishments in town. It's a talent she exploits with enthusiastic delight. But in her own gleaming kitchen, Connie is a stranger in paradise!

Still, like all of us, every now and again Connie is seized with the I-really-must-do-it-myself guilts. Thus, the genesis of this terrific dish. If Connie could muddle it out, so can you.

Ingredients

2 lbs. (1 kg) ground beef
1 large onion, sliced
2 tablespoons (30 mL) ketchup
1 tablespoon (15 mL) soya sauce
dash garlic powder
1 10 oz. (300 mL) can cream of mushroom soup
1 can small carrots
1 can whole or sliced potatoes

Method

Spread the onions over the bottom of an oven dish which has been greased with a non-stick spray. Mix up the ground beef, ketchup, soya sauce and garlic powder and mold into a loaf which you place on top of the onions. Surround this with the carrots and potatoes and then pour the soup over all. Bake at 350°F (180°C) for 1 hour.

Serve with a boxed instant noodle mix and Greek Salad (see p.85).

It's a cinch to muddle through and a sure, easy winner.

Piccadilly Meatballs

Serves 3-4

A touch of sweet, a tang of piquant, Piccadilly Meatballs make a sensational hot hors d'oeuvre or elegant entrée. Even a novice can stir up this storm.

Ingredients

2 lbs. (1 kg) ground beef
seasoning to taste (garlic powder, salt and pepper)
1 egg
1 10 oz. (300 mL) jar grape jelly
1/2 small bottle chili sauce (add more if necessary)
lemon juice to taste (start with 1/4 cup — 50 mL)

Method

Mix the meat, seasoning and egg, and set to one side. Simmer the other ingredients in a pot on the stove at medium heat. Add the meat, first forming it into walnut-size balls. Keep it all simmering until the meatballs are done (about 1/2 hour).

Serve in a smashing chafing dish and, if it is to be a main course, pour over instant long grain rice. Accompany with fresh cooked asparagus or broccoli spears.

Swedish meatballs from Canada

Serves 4 as a main dish;
serves 12 as an hors d'oeuvre (doubles easily)

What else can you do with ground beef? Here's an alternative that looks and tastes as though you really have flair. As a meal, served on instant long grain rice, it's delectable. As an hors d'oeuvre in a gleaming chafing dish or casual fondue pot, it bespeaks a talent for entertaining elegantly. And for ease, it can't be outdone.

Swedish Meatballs From Canada — how cosmopolitan can you get?

Ingredients

1-3/4 lbs. (800 g) ground beef
1 egg
1/2 cup (125 mL) bread crumbs or wheat germ
seasoning to taste (garlic powder, salt and pepper)
1 10 oz. (300 mL) can tomato soup
1 cup (250 mL) brown sugar
1/4 cup (50 mL) lemon juice

Method

Mix the meat, egg, bread crumbs (or wheat germ) and seasoning, and set aside. Simmer the other ingredients in a medium-sized pot on the stove and add the meat, first forming it into small balls. Simmer the whole thing for 3/4 hour on a low heat, and taste. This should be a sweet and sour taste sensation, so if it needs more brown sugar or lemon juice, adjust accordingly. Don't be afraid to add too much; you can always balance again by putting in a little more of the opposite flavor. It's foolproof artistry.

Take the few minutes necessary to make Marinated Cucumbers (see p.91) and your table's complete.

CROWN ROAST of lamb

(for an affair to remember…)
2-3 bones per person

Every once in a while, a gracious hostess is called upon to do something spectacular. That may mean anything from playing Beethoven's fifth on the crystal, to providing a truly superior dish for very special guests. Since we are concerned here with culinary skill, we will eliminate the musical tidbits at the outset and concentrate on a brilliantly performed entrée — Crown Roast of Lamb.

Don't be frightened by the enormity of the challenge ahead of you. It's merely a matter of courting your friendly butcher. Tell him how many guests you are planning to serve, and ask him to prepare a crown roast for that number. If he's half worth his hatchet, it will be his pleasure (but you should give him some advance notice so that he'll have your cut available).

Now you are ready to secure a lovely round silver tray. For some psychological reason, the setting adds immeasurably to the taste appeal of your offering, and scouting around for the perfect serving platter will prove well worth the effort. This having been done, you are ready to be sensational.

Ingredients

1 crown roast of lamb
1/2 cup (125 mL) Italian salad dressing
dash garlic powder
Stove Top stuffing

Method

Preheat the oven to 450°F (230°C), but lower to 350°F (180°C) when you put the lamb in. Protect the ends of the bones by covering them with aluminum foil. Baste the lamb well with the salad dressing (letting it stand in the dressing an hour or two is even better) and sprinkle with garlic powder. Roast 1/2 hour to the pound (65 minutes /kg) for well done, or 25 minutes (55 minutes /kg) for rare. (A meat thermometer may well help to steady your nerves if you have doubts to conquer.) Baste the lamb with the dressing and juices once or twice while it is roasting. One-half hour before it is done, remove the roast and fill the cavity with the stuffing you have prepared according to package directions — a nice addition here is to chop in some raw apple. Protect the stuffing from drying out by covering it with foil. Return to the oven for the remaining 1/2 hour.

Serve on your silver platter and garnish the legs with paper panties or super-huge stuffed olives. The entire rack should sit on a mass of green leaf lettuce with ripe cherry tomatoes scattered around.

Accompany with Asparagus Salad (see p. 89) or Classic Caesar Salad (see p. 84).

Leg of lamb royale

Serves 4

A shapely leg of lamb will elicit lewd remarks from the men and raves from the women. Properly presented, it has "a touch of royalty", for it used to be a favorite princely dish.

The tempting aroma of young spring lamb cooking unpretentiously in a commoner's roasting pan, then served with regal aplomb, may indeed be your crowning achievement.

Ingredients

1   5 or 6 lb. (2.5 kg to 3 kg) leg of lamb
1 bottle Italian salad dressing
2 cans small, whole boiled potatoes
1 or 2 cans whole baby carrots
1/2 cup (125 mL) dry red wine or white wine (optional)

Method

Remove the papery outer covering from the leg and then marinate it in the salad dressing (and wine if you wish) for several hours at least (or, better still, overnight). Turn the leg occasionally so that it gets the benefit of the dressing from all angles. When you're ready, place the leg in an open roasting pan and surround it with the vegetables. Pour a little of the dressing over them too…they're all in this together! Roast in a 350°F (180°C) oven for 2-1/2 hours or use a meat thermometer to sedate a case of nerves if you want it done exactly to your own taste. And by the way, there's no harm in removing the lamb from the oven for a little while to slow down the cooking if cocktails are taking longer than you bargained for. In this case, a thermometer is really essential.

Serve the leg on a dazzling platter surrounded by the vegetables which have been nestling close and are now beautifully glazed. Mint jelly (any good brand will do) shimmering in a pretty silver container is a must as an accompaniment. You may even want to add steamed asparagus or Judy's Favorite Broccoli Soufflé (see p. 110).

It's a dinner fit for kings!

Cherry Ham Steaks

1 steak per person

It has often been said by lovers of food that food is a love offering. If that is so, one would most certainly want one's efforts to look sincere. This tasty recipe is so pretty and honest-looking that even though it takes just a few minutes to prepare, your guests will know you care.

As well as being picture-pretty, Cherry Ham Steaks is also the perfect dish for that intimate candlelight dinner for two. Emerge from the kitchen with this in hand, and you've got an evening's entertainment made — sincerely.

Ingredients

4 ham steaks
8 slices bacon
prepared white horseradish
1/4 cup (50 mL) cornstarch (scant)
1/2 teaspoon (2 mL) dry mustard
handful golden raisins
1 10 oz. (300 mL) jar red currant jelly

Method

Sauté the bacon and set aside. Bake the steaks at 350°F (180°C) for 1/4 hour, then remove them from the oven and crisscross 2 strips of bacon on each steak. Return to the oven for 10 minutes. Meanwhile, make the sauce by combining the other ingredients over a low heat in a saucepan, stirring continuously. When the mixture reaches a boil, remove it from the heat.

Place the ham steaks on a serving platter and pour the sauce over them. Snuggled together thus, floating in an intimate red sea and accompanied by a tart green salad and Sweet Potato Pie (see p. 106), your offering is ready to serve.

Quicker Ham Steaks

1 steak per person

If ham steaks make you happy, here's an even quicker way to make them party pretty and delightfully delicious.

Ingredients

4 ham steaks
canned pineapple rings
1 10 oz. (300 mL) jar red apple jelly or red currant jelly

Method

Broil steaks on both sides. When the second side is nearly ready, top each steak with a pineapple ring filled with a tablespoon or two (about 25 mL) of your choice of jelly and place under the broiler again until brown. Couldn't be quicker!

Serve with a Spinach Salad (see p. 87) or Cauliflower Salad (see p. 90) and Potato Pudding Muffins (see p. 104).

VANCOUVER SPARE RIBS

3/4 - 1 lb. (350 g - 500 g) per person

It is well known to connoisseurs of good food that the women of western Canada have developed a rare and enviable skill in the art of cooking. I am convinced that this happy evolution occurred as a result of past generations being forced to invent their own dump recipes using whatever they had on hand.

Though many of these secret recipes are totally peculiar to the western setting and never see candlelight beyond the Rockies, I was fortunate to obtain, by way of my dear Aunt Shirley (a super cook who could never keep a secret), this delectable recipe.

I must admit that Vancouver Spare Ribs call for 20 minutes preparation time. However, that 20 minutes is spent in doing nothing more than watching the ribs boil (euphemistically called parboiling). And watching time doesn't count as working time, which is why I've let this one crawl under the "instant" wire. This dish promises a special taste sensation, and after the parboiling bit, it's simply another run-of-the-mill great dump recipe.

If you happen to have a ceramic oven dish, bake and serve in that.

Ingredients

spare ribs to suit number of guests
1 8 or 9 oz. (250 mL) jar marmalade
1 packet dehydrated onion soup
1/2 cup (125 mL) molasses
garlic powder to taste
orange slices (optional)

29

Method

Parboil the spare ribs for 20 minutes. When this is done, remove the ribs and drain for a few moments on paper towelling. Then place them in the oven dish and cover them with a mixture of all the other ingredients (except the orange slices). Bake at 325°F (160°C) for 1 hour.

Serve in the oven dish and garnish with orange slices. (For a little extra zing, you may add the orange slices for the last 10 minutes of baking.)

Potato Puffs Panache (see p. 105) and Spunky Pears (see p. 92) make nice accompaniments.

Adam's Ribs

Serves 4

Entertaining elegantly needn't be expensive. If you can keep the cost of your main dish from skyrocketing, you just may be able to maintain a down-to-earth budget. And a good way to begin is with Adam's Ribs. They aren't astronomical in cost, and they taste like a whole new world.

Ingredients

3 to 4 lbs. (1.5 kg to 2 kg) ribs (choose your favorite kind)
garlic powder to taste
1 cup (250 mL) brown sugar
1/4 cup (50 mL) corn syrup
2 to 3 tablespoons (30 mL to 45 mL) soya sauce
1-1/2 cups (350 mL) water

Method

Cut the ribs into pieces and sprinkle liberally with garlic powder. Cover tightly and bake for 1 hour at 425°F (220°C). Pour off excess fat. Combine the other ingredients by bringing them to a boil over medium heat and then simmering them for 10 minutes, stirring occasionally. Pour over ribs and serve accompanied by Gorgeous Green Beans (see p. 113) and Sweet Potato Pie (see p. 106).

Beef Wellington

(a company knockout and pocket book bender)
Serves 8

Traditionally, Beef Wellington is considered too difficult a feat for anyone but the finest gourmet chef. Even a competent *sous chef* must be a little audacious to consider attempting this piece of artistry.

Let us now break with tradition. Let us be recklessly brave. Let us defy convention and prepare a superbly simple and elegantly effective Beef Wellington. Yes, it can be done, even by you, but you must swear not to tell how embarrassingly easy it is to make. When the kudos begin (and I promise they will) an understated "It was nothing" will suffice.

When you are prepared to put a second mortgage on the house because you are having THE BIG DINNER PARTY, you are ready for Beef Wellington. Indeed, it is so superior, it is guaranteed to convince even the most sceptical guest that you are capable of anything!

First it is necessary to have a heart-to-heart with your butcher. Only the very best filet roast, New York roast or beef tenderloin will qualify for this sensational entrée. Think of it as an investment; if the meat is prime, that is your security. You can count on lots of interest!

Ingredients

filet roast, New York roast or beef tenderloin (about 4 lbs. — 2 kg)
meat seasoning
1 package frozen pastry dough, defrosted
1 tin liver pâté
1 egg

32

Method

To season the meat you may either sprinkle it with garlic powder, seasoned salt and seasoned pepper, or paint it with a "dry garlic sauce" (a sort of seasoned soya sauce which comes in a bottle and is normally used for spare ribs), or use your own favorite seasoning for beef. Then roast the meat at 350°F (180°C) in a preheated oven for 3/4 hour. Remove from the oven and cool. Roll out the defrosted pastry dough into a rectangle of 14 inches by 16 inches, (35 cm by 40 cm). Cut off three narrow strips of dough lengthwise and save these for the decoration. Spread the pâté onto the rectangle of dough, leaving about 1 inch (2.5 cm) uncovered on the long sides and about 2 inches (5 cm) uncovered on the ends. Then place the cooled beef in the center of the dough, upside down. Pull the dough over the beef, pinching the join to seal it, fold the ends like a package and tuck on top. Turn the whole thing over onto a fresh and lightly greased roasting pan or cookie sheet. (The juices from the first pan would mess up the dough.)

Now, for the professional touch. Make a braid of the three saved strips of dough and place the braid on top lengthwise, tucking the ends under the roast. Paint the whole package with egg yolk and roast another 40 minutes at 350°F (180°C) for rare; 50 minutes for medium-rare. A meat thermometer will ensure it is done to your taste.

Serve this offering on a silver platter surrounded by red spiced apple rings and fresh green asparagus (steamed no more than 6 to 8 minutes) and accompany with Hangover Pears (see p. 115) and a Pink Cloud (see p. 101).

Marinated Smug Roast

Serves 6, generously

In the world of the average terrified dinner party giver, the thought of a marinade is unreasonably intimidating. Listen to the word: marinade. Sounds strong, doesn't it? It's too authoritative, too professional, almost frightening. There seems to be a nebulous undercurrent associated with it. It whispers insistently: "For skilled cooks only."

I used to buy marinades in packages, bottles, whatever, and align them on my shelf according to classification, as a sort of challenge I would one day rise to meet. It helped me believe that ultimately I too would achieve success as a sensational cook. Use them? Of course not. They were just there to make me try harder.

In reality, I discovered quite the opposite is true. A good marinade will cover a multitude of sins, disguising a less than tender piece of meat as very upper crust, and preseasoning the meat to make it something special indeed. Doesn't that sound like a great find?

It's time to pull yourself together and face the fiend. Marinated Smug Roast, when thinly sliced, is economical and impressively good.

Ingredients

1 rib eye roast, approximately 3 lbs. (1.5 kg)
1/2 12 oz. bottle (350 mL) bottle dry garlic sauce (sold for use on spare ribs)
1/2 cup (125 mL) dry white wine

Method

Use a glass or Pyrex bowl, or deep dish, and marinate the roast in the sauce and the wine for several hours, at least. Overnight is even better. Turn the meat a few times during that period when you think of it, just to make sure it's treated all over. When you're ready to roast it, pour off the excess marinade and roast in the oven at 350°F (180°C). Follow the usual rule of thumb for timing, that is, 20 minutes to the pound (45 minutes/kg) for rare (if the roast is small, add on an extra 20 minutes at the end for good measure) and 25 to 30 minutes (55 minutes/kg to 65 minutes/kg) for well done. Of course, a meat thermometer eliminates all the fun of guessing.

Serve the roast on a large meat platter surrounded by spiced pears or red rings of spiced apples, and a fresh green vegetable. Slice thinly at the table.

By the way, if you want to include potatoes with the roast, here's a trick that makes them really tasty and beautifully browned. Just open a tin or two of whole potatoes and dip them in the marinade, covering them all around. Then roast them right along with the meat.

Cookie's baked steak

Approximately 1/2 lb. (250 g) per person

Summer evenings and steak. Unquestionably, a marriage made in heaven. What could surpass the gentle aroma of lusty sirloins mingling with the softness of summer breezes? Who can deny the sensuality of whitened coals, their subtle flames licking at the willing beef? But summer, like many affairs of the heart, ends.

If you're longing to rekindle the flame in the winter months; if you've sworn off spending another dollar on steak, rather than involuntarily incinerating it under the broiler, this recipe is for you.

Let's face it. You simply cannot simulate a barbecue in your kitchen. But you don't have to forget about steak entirely. You just have to think about it differently. Cookie did. She put aside the distant tingling memories of the coals, the silent insistence of the flames and took a brief journey into the unknown — a baked steak!

Cookie's Baked Steak is so well dressed it will take you anywhere. Its charm is in its cosmopolitan elegance. Prepare to begin a swinging affair.

Ingredients

2 inch (5 cm) thick sirloin
meat seasoning
prepared mustard
1 small bottle chili sauce
1 can whole mushrooms
1 Spanish onion, sliced
1 green pepper, sliced

Method

Ask your butcher to cut you a terrific steak for 4 (or more if you wish) 2 inches (5 cm) thick. When you have it home, season the steak (see under *Method* p. 33) and spread mustard on both sides. Place it in a shallow baking dish or pan and cover it with the chili sauce. (Note here that if it is a smallish steak, you may not need the entire bottle to cover it; or, for that matter, the entire onion, etc.) Pour the drained mushrooms on top. Garnish with the onion rings and peppers.

Since this dish will take 1 hour to bake, it is a good idea to have it at the ready, and pop it into the oven while your guests are having their cocktails. When the time is right, put the steak in a preheated oven at 350°F (180°C) and bake with the door slightly ajar. Try not to mess it up when you transfer it to a large serving platter, and then garnish it delicately with fresh parsley sprigs and cherry tomatoes. Divide into serving portions and accompany (if you wish) with Noshers' Noodle Pudding (see p. 100).

Brisket buffet

3 lb. (1.5 kg) roast serves 6;
5 lb. (2.5 kg) roast serves 10 or more

Have I got a recipe for you! This one has got to be the easiest way I know to serve 10 people well and inexpensively. It's hearty, filling, pretty, and adaptable — you can adjust the number of guests it serves merely by changing the size of the brisket…not the whole recipe. It's super every time.

Brisket Buffet is also just about impossible to overcook, so it's ideal to leave in a pretimed oven while you go about more important things. Because it has its very own vegetable accompaniments, simply adding a tossed green salad or fresh green vegetable makes the feast complete. And it's a breeze to clean up because it's all in one pan. For a sit-down dinner or tasty buffet, this recipe's got your number!

Ingredients

5 lb. (2.5 kg) single brisket
2 cans whole potatoes
2 cans whole baby carrots
1 can whole mushrooms
1/4 cup (50 mL) soya sauce
1 packet dehydrated onion soup
1 cup (250 mL) water (or ginger ale)
dash ketchup
1/2 lemon
sprinkle of brown sugar (optional)

Method

Put the brisket in a heavy roasting pan and surround it with the canned vegetables. Pour the soya sauce on top of the roast and then sprinkle the dry onion soup mix and brown sugar (if you wish) over that. Pour the water (or ginger ale), lemon juice and some ketchup around, and then toss the squeezed lemon right in with the roast. Cover tightly and roast at 350°F (180°C) for 3 hours or more (you can't overdo!). When it's cooked, slice it, cover and return to the oven (for 1/2 hour or until your guests are ready) to keep hot and absorb the juices. Next, pour off the juices and serve as gravy.

On a suitable meat platter, place the roast, sliced and surrounded by the vegetables which are now glistening and hot from the roaster. Your whole meal is complete and a guaranteed success.

California beef stew

Serves 6

At my house, the mention of beef stew used to produce undisguised cries of dismay. It was what my connoisseurs-in-residence affectionately and aptly called a "glug" meal. But the irony is that beef stew is supposed to take hours to prepare and reap proportionate praise from shiny little faces eager to dig in — or so the ladies' magazines would have us believe. With my family, however, the scene never read the way it was written, and the producer was too often heard to cry in an offstage whisper: "Doesn't anybody want some?".

Yet beef stew still remains the best way to rescue otherwise unconquerable cuts of meat. Besides, it's hearty, filling and kind to the budget. So, to save my self-respect and my pocket book, I decided to try a new recipe given to me by a lovely lady from California. It was such a success, I want to share it with you.

Now, pay close attention because it's so ridiculously easy you're sure to think you've missed something. This is a stew that *does not* require chopping and browning onions. It *does not* demand messy carrot scraping, or even prissy potato peeling. It is simply a glorious dump recipe, kitchen tested by ordinary picky people and perfect for a finicky family. It's better still for a late night winter supper with ruddy-cheeked friends just in from a toboggan run and eager for something hot and yummy.

Ingredients

2 lbs. (1 kg) lean beef cut into bite-sized chunks
1   10 oz. (300 mL) can mushroom soup
1   10 oz. (300 mL) can cream of celery soup
1 can whole potatoes, drained
1 packet dehydrated onion soup

Method

Put the meat in an oven casserole dish. Mix all the other ingredients together and pour over the meat. Bake covered in a preheated oven at 350°F (180°C) for 2-1/2 hours.

Serve in simple bowls accompanied by warm loaves of French bread. That's it! And please note, this recipe is easily doubled.

Veal Fiesta

(a bit of kitchen witchery)
Serves 4

Every now and then, my "fantastically-organized-I-don't-know-how-she-does-it-all" life seems to get all tangled up, and the big myth appears about to be exposed. Don't tell anyone, but deep down I'm discreetly disorganized. In fact, I like to have a million things going at once and then I find myself frantically trying to tidy up loose ends. Amazingly, I usually manage to do that quite well, so nobody suspects the awful truth (or so I tell myself). And I carry on with my finger in a dozen proverbial pies, pretending with childlike stubbornness that being terribly organized is actually very basic to my character.

Yet, if I can spend an entirely frantic day and top it off by conjuring up an enchanting meal that looks as though it took hours of time and a fertile imagination, then perhaps I really am organized and don't have to pretend. The trick is a little kitchen witchery.

If all of this is too complicated to follow, don't despair. The magical recipe herein isn't. Maybe that's why it's one of my favorites.

Ingredients

4 good-sized veal cutlets, flattened and pounded by the butcher
1 cup (250 mL) flour seasoned heavily with seasoned salt, garlic
    powder and seasoned pepper
margarine
1 can plain spaghetti sauce
1 can button mushrooms, drained
1 package sliced Mozzarella cheese
1 green pepper
1 tomato

Method

Dip the cutlets in the seasoned flour and lightly brown in a skillet with margarine. That's all the work there is. From here on, it's a classic dump recipe, and particularly convenient because you have a choice of either carrying on with dinner straight away, or freezing the cutlets after frying them to save for an especially frantic day when you want to look organized.

In either case, the next step is to place the cutlets in a baking dish with no overlapping. Pour the spaghetti sauce over the cutlets. Then dump in the drained mushrooms. Tear the cheese slices up into strips and spread them on top. Slice a few green pepper rings and scatter them around, and slice the tomato into eighths and put two pieces on each cutlet. (See if anyone dares call you disorganized after that!)

Bake all of this uncovered in a 350°F (180°C) oven for 3/4 hour (if the cutlets are frozen, bake for 1 hour) and serve with a simple lettuce salad and chunks of Italian bread.

Côtelettes en papillotes à la judy

Serves 4

For a party pleaser, this dish goes a long way to make you look *fantastique*. It's worth the little bit of fiddle required to get it going right, so don't back off just because you don't speak French...let your entrée do it for you.

Ingredients

4 veal cutlets, flattened and pounded by the butcher
1 cup (250 mL) flour seasoned with seasoned salt and seasoned
  pepper
vegetable oil
1 14 oz. (400 mL) can tomato sauce
1/4 cup (50 mL) red wine
garlic powder to taste
8 shallots, chopped
handful stuffed olives, sliced
1 can sliced mushrooms
1 tomato, sliced in wedges

Method

Dredge the meat in the seasoned flour and brown lightly in a skillet with a little oil. Line a baking dish with aluminum foil, and place the pieces of veal in the foil. Add the wine to the tomato sauce and spoon over the veal. Sprinkle with garlic powder, the shallots, olive slices and mushrooms. Place a slice of tomato on each cutlet, and cover the baking dish tightly with foil. Bake at 325°F (160°C) for 1/2 hour.

Serve with a simple Spinach Salad (see p. 87) and quick long grain rice. *Une pièce de résistance!*

Mother's mock duck

Serves 2-3

Father has a weakness for duck, and mother a weakness for father. I suspect this dish was conceived in a moment of madness when mother wanted to turn father into a tender bird.

Ingredients

1-1/2 lbs. (700 g) flank steak, pounded to an even thickness
1-1/2 cups (350 mL) Stove Top stuffing
1/2 cup (125 mL) grated Parmesan cheese
3 tablespoons (45 mL) vegetable oil
1 10 oz. (300 mL) can tomato soup
1 10 oz. (300 mL) can golden mushroom soup
1 large onion, chopped
dash garlic powder
dash basil

Method

Combine the stuffing with the cheese and spread over the meat. Then roll up the steak and tie securely. Brown the outside briefly in oil. Place in a baking dish. Combine the other ingredients and pour over top. Cover well and bake at 350°F (180°C) for 2 hours or more, until tender, basting from time to time.

Serve with Jeannette's Tasty Baked Asparagus (see p. 112).

Aunt shirley's never fail peanut butter chicken
Serves 4

How do you entertain elegantly on a peanut butter pocket book? Why Peanut Butter Chicken, of course!

Though the combination may sound unusual, the preparation is so easy and the results are so tantalizingly good, you'll want to use this recipe often as a dependable and inexpensive favorite.

Ingredients

1 chicken cut into parts
1 small jar peanut butter (plain or crunchy, whichever you wish)
1/2 cup (125 mL) molasses
pinch cayenne pepper

Method

Place the chicken parts in a baking dish. Mix up the other ingredients and spoon over top. Bake at 350°F (180°C) for 1-1/2 hours and serve in the baking dish.

This entrée goes particularly well with baked sweet potatoes (you save energy when you do them along with the chicken) and a fresh green vegetable or Chilled Bean Salad (see p. 88).

MOTHER'S COMPANY CANDIED CHICKEN

Serves 4 (doubles easily)

Here's another chicken winner. It's perfect for special company or anytime you want to impress the folks with your talent. Try it soon and let your family know you love 'em!

Ingredients

1 chicken cut into parts
1 10 oz. (300 mL) jar apricot jam or orange preserves
1 packet dehydrated onion soup
1 bottle French salad dressing
1/2 cup (100 mL) almonds or peanuts (optional)

Method

Place the chicken parts in an oven dish handsome enough to serve in. Mix up all the other ingredients and pour over top. Bake for 1-1/4 hours at 350°F (180°C) and serve.

A side dish of instant long grain rice works beautifully with this savory combination of flavors. Add a fresh Spinach Salad (see p. 87) and you have another instant success.

Fried Chicken Elinor

2-3 pieces per person

Ingredients

chicken pieces
1 bottle Italian salad dressing
crushed Corn Flakes (either the boxed kind, or roll your own)
honey

Method

Dip the chicken pieces into the salad dressing, coating them well, and then dip them in the crushed Corn Flakes. Bake at 350°F (180°C) for 3/4 hour. Remove from the oven and drizzle honey over top. Return to the oven and bake another 20 minutes.

Gorgeous Green Beans (see p. 113) make the meal complete.

Apricot chicken dinner

2-3 pieces per person

This easy recipe creates a pleasing combination of flavors and textures and is always a hit at my house. And because it's so attractive, it adds the perfect touch to any party table, as the main course or as an enchanting addition to a large buffet.

Ingredients

2 or 3 lbs. — 1 kg to 1.5 kg (about 15) chicken pieces, as needed
1/2 teaspoon (2 mL) salt
2 tablespoons (25 mL) margarine, melted
1 large tin apricots (or peaches), with liquid
1 cup (250 mL) your favorite barbecue sauce
1 tablespoon (15 mL) lemon juice

Method

Salt the chicken and cover with the margarine. Bake at 350°F (180°C) for 1/2 hour in an oven-to-table baking dish. Drain the fruit, reserving 1/2 cup (100 mL) of the syrup, and combine this syrup with the barbecue sauce and lemon juice. Pour over the chicken and continue to bake for 1/2 hour. Now arrange the fruit on top, baste once, and bake for another 20 minutes.

Serve with a simple green salad for texture and color.

Catch-on Chicken

(So named because it's bound to catch on quickly at your house)
Serves 6 (easily halved)

Ingredients

12 chicken pieces
1/4 cup (50 mL) liquid honey
1 large can orange sections, with liquid
ginger
sesame seeds

Method

Some people prefer this dish when the chicken has been skinned, but it works well either way.

Arrange the chicken pieces in a roasting pan and cover them with honey, the orange sections and the juice from the can. Sprinkle liberally with ginger and sesame seeds, and bake for 1-1/4 hours at 350°F (180°C). Garnish with sliced tomatoes.

Serve with instant long grain rice cooked, not in water, but in apple juice with one diced apple tossed in.

Marvin's diet chicken

Serves 4

Marvin is on a diet. And like so many other people on the calorie kick, he had a difficult time finding a company dinner that wouldn't put him on the fat side of yesterday. Until he came up with this. It's easy, slimming, and mighty tasty too.

Ingredients

6 half chicken breasts
salt and pepper to taste
garlic powder to taste
1/4 cup (50 mL) soya sauce
1-1/2 cups (350 mL) tomato juice
4 tablespoons (50 mL) vinegar
onion flakes
2 packets sugar substitute

Method

Place the chicken breasts in a lightly sprayed baking dish, meat side down. Sprinkle with salt, pepper and garlic powder. Mix all the other ingredients and pour over top. Bake uncovered at 350°F (180°C) for 1 hour.

Serve with a tempting green salad topped with diet dressing, and spiced apple rings straight from the jar, or Hangover Pears (see p. 115). Your figure-conscious friends will love you!

Sticky Chicken Wings

Serves 4-5

Another chicken recipe? Why not? Chicken continues to wage war against inflation and has bravely survived as one of the last remaining cost-conscious entrées. Besides, while you're cudgeling your brain for alternatives to the red meat artery cloggers, you really need several marvelous chicken recipes.

Sticky Chicken Wings, a terrific "can"-do recipe, boasts a heaping display of tender young broiler wings gently glazed with your own delectable garlic and honey seasoning. It's finger stickin' delicious and easy enough for the novice.

Ingredients

3 lbs. — 1.5 kg (18 or so) small chicken wings
1 12 oz. (350 mL) bottle dry garlic sauce (sold for use on spare ribs)
4 or 5 tablespoons (50 mL to 75 mL) honey

Method

Place the wings in a large baking dish and bake uncovered for 1/2 hour at 350°F (180°C). Remove from the oven, pour off the fat and cover with the garlic sauce. Dribble the honey over top. Bake uncovered at 350°F (180°C) for at least 1 hour, turning the wings once to coat and brown them all over. They'll get nicely glazed and sticky, and if they're a little overdone, even better.

Serve with instant long grain rice to which canned sliced mushrooms and frozen peas have been added, or mix the rice with pineapple chunks.

Pay 'em back tuna casserole

Serves 3-4

Admit it. All of us, weak human creatures that we are, have some emotional reactions in common. If that bit of philosophizing sounds a little incongruous in a cook book, think again. Have you ever noticed how often an inexplicable emotional response revolves around food? I'll prove it to you.

Picture this: you drop into a friend's home for just a moment...perhaps to return a lost glove. Inconsequential. You get to chatting amiably and you find you have been persuaded to stay for lunch. "Pot luck" she calls it; "nothing special." You continue comfortably over a coffee and before your very eyes, your soon to be ex-friend whips up a fantasy or two. A remarkable repast! Though you are slightly in awe of this natural flair, you are curiously aware that you have developed a simultaneous instant hatred. It's the kind of intimidating incident over which tenuous friendships are broken — because somehow, you have to pay her back and make it look easy.

Call it a paradox of human nature, but in spite of developing an "instant hatred" for such a cunning creature, I want to copy her. When she drops in to return my missing mitten, I want to have a guaranteed smash hit immediately at hand to call "pot luck." An elegant luncheon of utmost simplicity. A dash of panache.

For such trying times, and for other times too, I keep four little cans always on my shelf. Individually they're unassuming but in combination they blend into a delicate casserole that can be whipped up at the drop of a glove. No talent needed...just four little cans.

53

Ingredients

2 7 oz. (200 g) tins tuna, drained and flaked
1 10 oz. (300 mL) can mushroom soup
1 can tender little peas
1 cup (250 mL) crushed potato chips
two pieces of toast

Method

Combine all the ingredients, except for the potato chips and toast, and pour into a small buttered casserole dish. (You may want to save some dish washing time by mixing the ingredients in the serving casserole itself.) Top with the crushed potato chips (just roll them between your hands). If you haven't got chips, Corn Flakes will do. And if you're out of Corn Flakes, try crushed pretzels or even soda crackers. Bake in a 350°F (180°C) oven for 1/2 hour. Remove from the oven and tuck toast triangles (i.e., toast cut diagonally) around the casserole to complete the effect. Alternatively, serve in patty shells.

A pot of steaming coffee adds the finishing touch. You may want to keep two especially pretty placemats with matching linen napkins at the ready for just such a little luncheon.

ANOTHER TUNA CASSEROLE

Serves 2-3

If you have a few minutes to dawdle, this is a nice variation of the Pay 'Em Back Tuna Casserole. It's much the same, but you include a bunch of flat egg noodles for character, do away with the toast and potato chips, and you may omit the peas if you wish.

Ingredients

1 7 oz. (200 g) tin of tuna, drained and flaked
1/2 bag flat egg noodles
1 10 oz. (300 mL) can mushroom soup

Method

Boil the noodles according to package directions and drain them well. Place 1/2 in a buttered casserole or baking dish, and reserve 1/2 for the top. Cover the noodles with the tuna and then pour the soup over top. Crown with remaining noodles and bake for 1/2 hour at 350°F (180°C).

Serve with a lettuce salad for a simple and simply elegant meal.

Tuna joy

Serves 4

I promise you, this is the last tuna casserole, and probably the best. It's as simple as the others, but there seems to be a little more magic in the combination of ingredients.

Ingredients

2 7 oz. (200 g) tins of tuna, drained and flaked
1 10 oz. (300 mL) can mushroom soup
handful salted peanuts
3/4 cup (175 mL) Chinese egg noodles (dry type)
celery stalk, chopped very fine

Method

Mix all the ingredients in a buttered casserole dish. Bake at 350°F (180°C) for 1/2 hour or until bubbling nicely, then spread a little joy around!

Adding a salad is nice, but this dish is really complete all on its own.

Salmon Steaks Supreme, or Halibut Heaven

Serves 4

This marvelous creation comes from an inventive college student I once knew who made his way through the Ivy League maze by trading cooking and light housekeeping duties in exchange for room and board. He invariably conned an already financially overburdened professor into the arrangement and was, therefore, expected to manage brilliantly on a meagre budget. It became an imperative personal challenge to stretch a buck as far as it would go, so as not to curtail his own social life.

As a result, my college comrade created several money-saving numbers which looked great for small but elegant dinner parties, and left a little bit over for under-the-table-trysts. This is one of my favorites.

Unfortunately, inflation has caught up with the plucky little salmon, removing it indefinitely from the inexpensive category. But this recipe works as well with halibut.

Ingredients

4 salmon or halibut steaks
seasoned flour
margarine
cottage cheese (small curd type)

Method

Dip the steaks lightly in the flour which you have seasoned to taste (try adding seasoned salt and a little lemon pepper). Place the steaks on a broiling pan and dot with margarine. Broil 7 or 8 minutes, until lightly browned. Turn the steaks over and broil about 3 minutes. Then remove them from the broiler for a moment while you spread them generously with the cottage cheese. Broil again until the cheese melts and is lightly browned.

Serve on an attractive tray lined with huge lettuce leaves and lavishly garnished with parsley and tomato wedges, and add a Chilled Bean Salad (see p. 88).

Super Salmon Steaks

Serves 4

From the West, here is an unusual but delightful fish recipe you'll want to try soon. It boasts an enchanting combination of flavors and super simple preparation.

Ingredients

4 salmon steaks
1 bag of Cheezies
2 eggs
butter

Method

Take a handful of Cheezies and crush them up (crush more as you need them). Dip each salmon steak, first in the eggs which have been lightly beaten with a fork, and then in the crushed Cheezies. Fry in butter.

Serve on a pretty platter well dressed with lettuce leaves and tomato wedges. Add Judy's Favorite Broccoli Soufflé (see p. 110) and some easy oven rolls, and you've got a polished and colorful entrée.

Salmon Marcelle

Serves 6

Use salmon steaks or whole salmon — it's perfect either way. The ingredients in the following recipe are for 1/2 a salmon. Ask your fish man to butterfly it and discard the bone.

Ingredients

1/2 salmon
dash salt and pepper
1 pint (500 mL) commercial sour cream
1 10 oz. (300 mL) can tomato soup
3 large onions, sliced
1 lemon

Method

Place the salmon on a piece of triple-thick aluminum foil (cut large enough to wrap the salmon up tight). Sprinkle with salt and pepper. Pour the sour cream and the soup over the salmon and scatter the onions. Slice a lemon and place it on top for added zing. Wrap it all up well and seal. Bake at 325°F (160°C) for 3/4 hour.

Serve on a gorgeous platter bedded with lots of leaf lettuce and sprigs of fresh parsley strewn here and there for effect. Classic Caesar Salad (see p. 84) complements this dish nicely.

Helene's super sweet and sour salmon
Serves 2-3 (doubles easily)

Here's a dynamite fish dish you can toss together in seconds and serve any way you please. It's a refreshing salad, an inviting addition to any buffet table or, served with crackers, a tantalizing appeteaser. Make as much as you need by adjusting the ingredients appropriately. Since all the measurements are approximate, just mess around a little until it tastes exactly right to you.

Ingredients

1 8 oz. (250 g) tin salmon, drained and flaked
1/2 cup (125 mL) crushed pineapple, drained
1/2 cup (125 mL) slivered almonds
2 tablespoons (25 mL) mayonnaise
curry powder to taste

Method

Mix everything together and serve cold on a fresh bed of leaf lettuce. Frozen croissants (the kind you simply pop into the oven) are an elegant addition.

61

JOANNE'S SUNDAY MORNING QUICHE

Serves 4

Sunday morning or any time, this quiche cousin makes an impressively easy and simply delicious meal. Just assemble the ingredients, pile 'em up, and you've got it made.

Ingredients

4 slices egg bread (*challah*)
3 eggs
1 7 oz. (200 g) tin tuna or salmon, drained and flaked.
1 can mushroom bits, drained
ketchup
grated cheese (any kind you have handy)

Method

Line a lightly sprayed Pyrex dish with the bread after trimming off the crust. Whip the eggs with a little milk (using a fork or, better still, a beater for a moment), and spread over the bread. Then spread the tuna or salmon on top, cover with the mushrooms, add a few dots of ketchup, and sprinkle the whole thing with cheese. Bake for about 1/2 hour at 350°F (180°C).

Perk a pot of coffee and that's it!

Shrimp Stroganoff

Serves 4-6

Elegant company coming, and you want to knock them off their feet? Try this luxurious blend of rich noodles and tender seafood in a tantalizing sauce — it's a winner!

Ingredients

1 8 oz. (227 g) package medium-width egg noodles
1 lb. (500 g) frozen cooked shrimp, defrosted
3/4 cup (175 mL) commercial sour cream
1/4 cup dry sherry
1 clove garlic, finely minced
1 teaspoon (5 mL) chopped parsley
1/4 teaspoon (1 mL) Worcestershire sauce
grated Swiss cheese
salt and pepper to taste

Method

Boil the noodles according to package directions and drain well. Mix in all the other ingredients except the cheese. Pour into a buttered casserole, and sprinkle the cheese on top. Bake in a 325°F (160°C) oven for 1/2 hour, and serve with a Spinach Salad (see p. 87) for accompaniment.

Marcia's boston lobster

Serves 2

For an intimate dinner of pure pleasure, luxuriate in the extravagance of stuffed lobster. The drama of "candlelight only" handsomely completes the scene.

Ingredients

2 fresh lobsters, split lengthwise by the fishman
1/2 cup (100 mL) bread crumbs
2 handfuls Ritz crackers, crushed
dash sherry
1/4 lb. (125 g) chopped scallops
1/4 teaspoon (1 mL) garlic powder (more if you like)
tomalley from lobster (the green stuff)
butter

Method

Stuff the lobsters with all the other ingredients which you have mixed well in a bowl. Dot with butter and wrap in aluminum foil. Bake 25 minutes at 450°F (230°C), then unwrap and bake at 400°F (200°C) without the foil for another 20 minutes (or until nicely browned).

Serve with garlic bread and a snappy green salad.

Pot o' shellfish

Serves 4-6

When you need a make-it-now-serve-it-later specialty, Pot O'Shellfish fills the bill. It'll wait until you and your guests are in the mood to be delighted. Perfect for after ski, after sun, or after anything.

Ingredients

8 oz. (200 g) elbow macaroni
1   10 oz. (300 mL) can cream of mushroom soup
1 cup (250 mL) milk
1   8 oz. (250 g) tin crab meat, well drained
1 small tin shrimp, well drained
1 green pepper, diced
1 small can mushrooms
pepper and garlic salt to taste
2 to 3 tablespoons (30 mL to 45 mL) grated Parmesan cheese
butter

Method

Make the macaroni according to package directions. Heat the soup and milk and add macaroni and other ingredients, except for the cheese and butter. Put into 6 individual baking dishes, or 1 large casserole dish. Sprinkle with the cheese and dot with butter. Heat in a 350°F (180°C) oven for 1/2 hour and then brown under the broiler for a few moments.

Serve with a green salad and a pot of steaming coffee.

Almost great baked fish

Serves 6

I have known clever people who gleefully gobble anything that swims because they say fish supplies food for the brain. However, I suspect they simply love seafood.

Without a doubt, fish, high in protein and low in fat, is an incredible edible. So, for fish fanciers everywhere, I have included this dish. It's simple, it's delightful...in fact, it's almost great!

Ingredients

2-1/2 lbs. (1.25 kg) white fish, sole, perch or Boston bluefish filets
1/4 lb. (125 g) butter or margarine
1/3 cup (75 mL) chopped frozen onion
dash salt
1   10 oz. (300 mL) can tomato soup

Method

Absorb the excess moisture from the fish with paper towelling and place the filets in a baking dish. Sprinkle with the onion, dot with the butter, salt to taste, and pour the soup over everything. Bake at 350°F (180°C) for 3/4 to 1 hour, or until the fish flakes easily.

Served with a tangy salad and perhaps a side dish of corn, this is a lovely variety of color and taste sensations (not to mention a healthy offering of brain food).

Lemon butter baked fish

Serves 4

Ingredients

1 box (1 lb. — 500 g) frozen fish filets, defrosted
1/4 lb. (125 g) margarine
1/3 cup (75 mL) bottled lemon juice

Method

Blot the excess moisture from the fish and place in a baking dish. Dot with the margarine and cover with the lemon juice. Bake at 350°F (180°C) for about 3/4 hour or until the fish is easily flaked.

Simple accompaniments do just fine here — Chilled Bean Salad (see p. 88) or a green salad, and possibly corn or sweet potatoes for starch. Homemade rolls (the packaged freezer compartment kind) are a must, with pots of fresh butter.

Roll over sole

approximately 2 filets per person

Here's a recipe that makes its own delicate sauce so simply, it looks as though you took lessons from Escoffier. Perfect for company, it readily doubles, trebles, or maxi-multiplies. And served in gleaming silver, it makes any meal an event.

Ingredients

filets of sole, as needed, blotted dry
milk
1 tablespoon (15 mL) mayonnaise
1/2 cup (100 mL) ketchup
salt
processed Cheddar cheese slices (1 for every 2 filets)

Method

Add enough milk to the mayonnaise to make 1/2 cup (100 mL). Combine with the ketchup. Set aside. Salt each filet, top with 1/2 slice of cheese, roll up jellyroll-style. Secure with a toothpick. Place in a buttered baking dish and pour the mayonnaise mixture over top. Bake at 350°F (180°C) for 3/4 hour.

Serve with Chilled Bean Salad (see p. 88) and Sweet Potato Pie (see p. 106).

Stuffed pepper boats

Serves 4

With prices forever shooting up, who among us does not look for a budget cutter that isn't a downer? Once in a while you may come across a winner, just as you are doing now — and aren't you glad it's easy too?

Ingredients

2 large green peppers
1/2 cup (100 mL) (approximately) white rice
1/2 lb. (250 g) Cheddar cheese, cubed
1   10 oz. (300 mL) can cream of tomato soup (or 1-1/4 cups —
    300 mL — Ragú spaghetti sauce)

Method

Cook the rice according to package directions, to measure 1-1/4 cups (300 mL) when cooked. Cut the peppers in half lengthwise and remove the seeds. Parboil 5 minutes. Then combine the rice, cheese and 1/2 the tomato soup (or spaghetti sauce), mixing well, and stuff into the pepper cavities. Place the peppers in a shallow oven-to-table baking pan and cover and surround with the remaining soup. Bake at 350°F (180°C) for 1/2 hour.

Serve with French sticks, and your meal is complete at a cost you can celebrate.

Soups

Thick and chunky cheater's chowder

Serves 6 as a main dish;
Serves a lot more as an appetizer

The average busy cook thinks of chowder, if she thinks of it at all, as too time-consuming to include in her repertoire of soup recipes. But Cheater's Chowder can be thrown together in a few minutes and is really too good to miss. It takes a lot of dumping, a little simmering, and serves up wonderfully homemade tasting. It's just right for a cold winter luncheon or evening meal, especially if it's presented in a huge steaming tureen with baskets of thick French stick and pots of butter.

Ingredients

1 10 oz. (300 mL) can cream of celery soup
1 10 oz. (300 mL) can fish or seafood chowder
1 can sliced potatoes
1-1/2 cups (350 mL) milk or cream (or more if you want to stretch
   the soup)
2 tablespoons (30 mL) butter
1 tin clams, crab meat or lobster chunks, well drained, or even 1/2
   lb. (250 g) frozen or fresh fish filets cut into chunks…in other
   words, any kind of fish you like.

Method

Mix all the ingredients together in a heavy covered pot and simmer on the stove for 1 hour.

Jack's tomato soup cream dream

Makes as much as you want!

An artist friend of mine, a multi-talented, many-faceted man whose skills also include cooking, generously offered to share this recipe with me so that I might pass it on to you. If you're striving for mastery in the instant arts, you deserve this little dream.

Tomato Soup Cream Dream boasts a rich and creamy combination of delicate Italian seasoning and saucy tomato. And courtesy of a never-fail happy cooker, it's all yours. Serve it hot or cold, but serve it! Soon.

Ingredients

Ragú spaghetti sauce
cream

Method

Combine equal amounts of sauce and cream. Either chill and serve or heat and serve. One way or the other, it's a knockout.

Blitz crab bisque

Serves 6-8

Ingredients

1 8 oz. (250 g) tin crab meat, drained and flaked
3 tablespoons (45 mL) sherry
1 tablespoon (15 mL) Worcestershire sauce
1 10 oz. (300 mL) can split pea soup
1 10 oz. (300 mL) can tomato soup
1/2 cup (100 mL) cream
3/4 cup (175 mL) bouillon

Method

Soak the crab meat in the sherry and Worcestershire sauce for 5 minutes. Meanwhile, combine the pea soup and tomato soup, and heat to boiling. In another pot on the stove heat the cream and mix in the bouillon, then stir this into the soup mixture. Add the crab meat and heat, but keep below boiling.

Chilled TOMATO borscht

Serves 2 (doubles easily)

Ingredients

1 14 oz. (400 mL) can tomato juice
1 cup (250 mL) commercial sour cream
1 egg, hard-boiled

Method

To chilled juice add the sour cream and mix well. When serving, garnish with slices of hard-boiled egg.

European cabbage borscht

Serves…don't ask! (makes a lot)

Before I became an ardent advocate of easy elegance, I used to collect long and complicated recipes. I even tried a few, among them a cabbage borscht or two. All that time and energy spent steaming and doctoring up a cabbage gave me a feeling of earning my keep.

Then I discovered that it was actually possible (no, correct that — better) to dump my cabbage borscht. So I eliminated all the steaming and draining nonsense and went right to the heart of the matter…I just dumped it and let it do its thing. And may I add, it does it rather well.

Ingredients

1 medium to large cabbage, sliced fine
1 lb. (500 g) flank steak, cut into chunks
2 20 oz. (600 mL) cans tomato juice
1 medium can stewed tomatoes (including juice)
3 beef bouillon cubes
1 cup (250 mL) brown sugar
1/3 cup (75 mL) lemon juice
2 or 3 soup bones (optional)

Method

Put all the ingredients into your biggest pot, and bring to a boil. Turn down the heat and wait approximately 5 minutes for a froth to form on top. Skim this off with a spoon, and turn the heat to a low simmer. Cover the pot, leaving a little space for the steam to escape, and simmer for about 2 hours. (I know this doesn't sound quick, but the amount of preparation time involved is about 5 minutes, which is as fast as you can get for a real old-fashioned European borscht.)

After about 2 hours, taste it. You will probably notice that it is a little too sweet or somewhat too tart for your liking, so simply adjust the seasoning by adding either more brown sugar or lemon juice. Don't be afraid…you can't overdo. Too much of one is easily balanced by adding more of the other and it all adds immeasurably to the richness of the flavor. When you've got it just right, leave it to simmer for another hour or so, until the cabbage is tender.

Your cabbage borscht is now ready to serve, or to be put away to reheat another time, or even to be frozen (which it does so well, you'll be sorry you didn't make a double batch to divide up and store for another instant meal).

Of course you may serve the borscht as a starter to a terrific meal, but on a cold and lazy day, nothing could be better than a lusty bowlful of steaming borscht served as a meal in itself, with thick black bread and lots of butter. You can bet they never had it this good in Europe!

Make it easy homemade soup

Serves 10-12

I can't lie about it — this one takes time. Not much effort, mind you, but time. However, if you yearn for the finest, old-fashioned European-style thick and yummy homemade soup (the kind that's perfect to send to a sick mother-in-law, just to let her know how well you treat her son), it may be worth a little investment. And since there's no pot watching required, you can easily make it any time you have something else to do around the house. It also freezes like a dream, and so can be divided up and stashed away for emergencies.

Ingredients

1 packet dehydrated Jewish-style vegetable or barley and bean
   soup
4 beef bouillon cubes
3 marrow or soup bones
3 carrots, chopped or sliced
1 can potatoes, drained and quartered (or use raw potatoes, which
   are better but more time consuming)
any other raw vegetable you may wish to add
1 strip short ribs (optional)

Method

Do *not* follow soup packet instructions. Pour all the ingredients, except the potatoes (unless raw) into a Dutch oven (i.e., a big pot, about 6 qts.) which is about 3/4 full of boiling water. Turn the heat down to simmer, and after about 5 minutes skim off the foam on top. Now cover lightly (so that some steam can escape) and leave alone on a very low heat for about 3 hours. If using canned potatoes, add them about 1/2 hour before the soup's done, at which time you may also correct the seasoning by adding salt, if necessary.

Served with hot rolls and a tossed salad, it's a whole meal in itself.

Salad Samplers

Anyone can vivisect a head of lettuce and call it a salad. But you wouldn't call the effort a creative one, nor would you call the result an enticing addition to an elegant table.

Most salads are depressingly mediocre when a little imagination could make them what they really deserve to be — memorable complements to a perfect meal. A salad may even be the whole meal. But whichever, it should do three things: (1) add a dash of color, texture and pizazz, (2) fulfil your vitamin quota painlessly, and (3) show how talented you can be, even in the simple departments.

Almost any combination of fresh vegetables, cheese strips, meat or seafood will make a terrific salad if presented with confidence. Go wild! Make your own favorites into a fascinating blend of colors, textures and tastes. Add a simple dressing, or put two or three dressings into servers and let your guests make the final decision. Alternatively, offer a dazzling array of fresh edibles for a do-it-yourself salad bar. The following interesting variations will get you started.

Note: A good rule of thumb is to allow 1 head of lettuce for 4 people. However, with romaine lettuce, which often has tough outer leaves, you may have to adjust this and use your own judgement. For spinach salads, figure 1 bag for 3 people; as a side dish figure 1 bag for 5 to 6 people.

Classic CAESAR salad

Ingredients

2 or 3 heads romaine lettuce
1/4 to 1/2 bottle Caesar salad dressing
1/2 cup (125 mL) grated Parmesan cheese
1-1/2 teaspoons (7 mL) garlic powder
1 cup (250 mL) croutons (more if you wish)

Method

Wash and dry the lettuce well. Tear it into bite-sized pieces and discard the discolored bits and tough spines. Add the dressing and sprinkle with the cheese and garlic powder to make it taste homemade. Throw in the croutons and toss.

Serve immediately as an accompaniment, a separate course, or as an entrée for a light luncheon. It's always a classic!

Greek salad

Ingredients

1 head lettuce
1/2 cup (125 mL) black olives
1/2 lb. (250 g) feta cheese, crumbled
green pepper rings
tomato wedges
1/4 to 1/2 bottle Italian salad dressing
3 eggs, hard-boiled

Method

Wash and dry the lettuce well. Tear it up into bite-sized pieces. Add everything else (excepting the eggs, but including the dressing) and toss. Halve the eggs and decorate with them.

Julienne salad

Ingredients

1 head lettuce
shoestring strips of chicken, ham or bologna (or all of these)
shoestring strips of cheese (American and brick make a good
   combination)
3 eggs, hard-boiled and cut in wedges
red pepper rings

Method

Wash and dry the lettuce well. Tear it up into bite-sized pieces and
add all the other ingredients. You may wish to add, subtract or
substitute whatever cold meats you happen to have around, and it
will probably work equally well. Toss everything together in a big
wooden salad bowl, and serve as the main course for a luncheon.
Offer a selection of salad dressings on the side and perhaps some
croissants to complete the country feeling.

Spinach salad

It seems a fresh spinach salad is fast becoming "the" elegant luncheon entrée for the cognoscenti; perhaps because it's colorful, easy to prepare and, of particular importance in this era of health food faddists, loaded with wholesome goodies. Whatever the reasons, a spinach salad — and this one especially — is the perfect accent to any table.

Ingredients

1 or 2 bags spinach
3/4 cup (175 mL) bacon bits from a jar (or make your own)
1/2 lb. (250 g) fresh mushrooms, sliced
1 handful fresh bean sprouts
1 cup (250 mL) croutons (optional)
1 handful sunflower seeds (optional), shelled
1/4 to 1/2 bottle Italian or Caesar salad dressing
1 egg, hard-boiled

Method

Wash and dry the spinach discarding the bad pieces, and tear into bite-sized pieces. Toss all the ingredients, except for the dressing and the egg, together. Add the dressing and toss again. Grate the egg on top.

87

Chilled bean salad

Ingredients

1 can red kidney beans
1 can green beans, drained
1 can wax beans, drained
1/2 red onion, sliced into rings
1/2 cup (100 mL) Caesar or Italian salad dressing
1 can button mushrooms, drained (optional)
fresh cauliflower florets (optional)

Method

Dump the kidney beans into a sieve and run them under cold water for a moment to remove the excess juices. Shake dry. Then toss the beans and all the other ingredients (including the dressing) in a sparkling glass bowl. Chill before serving.

Asparagus salad

This vegetable dish makes a particularly attractive addition to a heavy meat meal, and because it's chilled, it also offers a pleasant change from the traditional hot stuff.

Ingredients

bunch of fresh asparagus
1/2 to 1 lb. (250 g to 500 g) fresh mushrooms, sliced
1/4 to 1/2 bottle Italian or Caesar salad dressing

Method

Steam the asparagus briefly (no more than 5 or 6 minutes). Drain well and place in a handsome serving dish. Add the mushrooms and the salad dressing, and chill for several hours.

Cauliflower salad

Ingredients

1 cauliflower
1 green pepper, sliced
1 red pepper, sliced
2 celery sticks, chopped
2 green onions, chopped
1/4 to 1/2 bottle Italian salad dressing
pepper to taste
grated Parmesan cheese to taste

Method

(This is probably best using the cauliflower in its raw state, but you may steam it briefly first if you wish.) Wash the cauliflower, break it into florets and discard the core. Then add all the other goodies and chill.

Marinated cucumbers

Ingredients

1 large cucumber
salt to taste
2 or 3 onions, chopped
1/2 cup (100 mL) vinegar
1-1/2 tablespoons (20 mL) sugar

Method

Slice the cucumber thinly and sprinkle with salt. Combine with the chopped onion. Mix the sugar and vinegar and pour over the cucumber and onion. Chill for several hours before serving.

Spunky Pears

Ingredients

leaf lettuce or watercress
canned pear halves (figure 1/2 pear per person with a few extras
   for second helpings), drained
1 small jar mint jelly

Method

Dress a flat platter with the lettuce or watercress and make an
arrangement of the pear halves, hollow side up. Fill the hollow with
a dash of mint jelly and chill before serving. Luxuriously refreshing
with a heavy meal.

PINEAPPLE CHEESE RING

Ingredients

1 small can crushed pineapple, well drained
3 4 oz. (100 g) packages cream cheese
1 small jar maraschino cherries
1/4 pint (150 mL) whipping cream, whipped

Method

Mix the pineapple with the softened cream cheese and add as many sliced cherries as you like for color. Fold in the whipped cream. Press into a mold and freeze.

To serve, unmold onto a heap of leaf lettuce and garnish with fresh mint leaves. Allow to defrost. By the way, it's also delightful when filled with fresh fruit and served as a luncheon dish.

GREEN PEPPER AND CHEESE PLEASE

Here's an unusual duet that's gaily colored and makes a tempting side dish or little luncheon.

Ingredients

green peppers (1 per person)
4 oz. (100 g) cream cheese (sufficient for 2 peppers)
3 oz. (85 g) bag chopped walnuts

Method

Wash and core the peppers, removing all the seeds. Soften the cheese and mix with the nuts according to your taste. Stuff the peppers solidly with this mixture and chill. Before serving, slice into wedges and arrange on watercress or lettuce leaves, either on individual salad plates or on one large, lovely platter.

POINSETTIAS

Ingredients

tomatoes (1 per person)
4 oz. (100 g) cream cheese (sufficient for 4 tomatoes)
1/2 cup (125 mL) commercial sour cream
dash paprika

Method

Slice the tomatoes into eighths, not cutting all the way through, so they look like flowers. Mix the cream cheese with the sour cream and drop a dollop into the center of each tomato. Sprinkle with paprika and serve on crisp lettuce for a colorful addition to any entrée.

Tuna salad sensation

Ingredients

2 7 oz. (200 g) tins tuna, drained and flaked
1 can water chestnuts, well drained
1 green pepper, chopped
3 stalks celery, chopped chunky
1 can pineapple chunks, well drained
mayonnaise to moisten
curry powder to taste

Method

Mix all the ingredients. Serve with croissants and perhaps a tomato juice cocktail.

Side Dishes and Snicklesnackles

Having won the battle of the main dish does not necessarily mean you are about to win the war. All too often, an enterprising host or hostess will find that after tucking the entrée easily into the oven, he or she is suddenly stumped for appropriate accompaniments. What to serve pre, peri and post may be your biggest problem.

If you're out to wow 'em (and we've already admitted to that plan of attack) your main plate is only the beginning. Your selection of side dishes can make the difference between adequate eating and gracious dining.

The following few pages include a tempting collection of side dishes and snicklesnackles. They were gathered here and there from professionals (who make everything look easy) and from friends with flair (who are learning to). I've lumped them all together because the uses to which these recipes can be put are limited only by your imagination — many are perfect as canapés, but work equally well as side dishes or appetizers. And they're all far easier than elegance has any right to be!

Nosher's noodle pudding

(a sweet addition to any meal)

This dish freezes particularly well, but if you plan to do so, it's a good idea to bake for only 1/2 the regular time before freezing. Then, when you need it, defrost and bake for 3/4 hour. It's ready when you are!

Ingredients

Pudding
10 oz. (300 g) medium egg noodles
2 eggs
2 cups (500 mL) buttermilk
1/3 cup (75 mL) white sugar
1 small can fruit cup or diced apricots, drained, or 1/2 cup (125 mL) golden raisins (or both fruit and raisins)

Topping
1 cup (250 mL) crushed Corn Flakes
1/4 cup (50 mL) brown sugar
1/4 cup (50 mL) melted butter

Method

Boil the noodles in salted water for 7 minutes, and drain. Then mix in a bowl with all the other pudding ingredients. Pour into a buttered oven dish. Mix the topping ingredients together and pour over the pudding. Bake at 350°F (180°C) for 1 hour.

Pink cloud

Ingredients

1/2 pint (250 ml) whipping cream
1 small jar red horseradish

Method

Whip the cream until stiff. Fold in the horseradish, a spoonful at a time, until the mixture turns a smashing pink. Serve alongside any beef dish for dazzle.

Stuffing stuff

It's true that you can use the easy-make stuffings on the market and get along fine. But if you really want to impress 'em, here's a scratch recipe that's so easy, it's almost too good to pass up. Perfect for fowl, it also works well with lamb.

Ingredients

1 pint (500 mL) tart apple sauce
1 cup (250 mL) bread crumbs
1/2 cup (100 mL) frozen chopped onion
dash powdered sage
dash cayenne pepper

Method

Just mix, and stuff.

Russell's party pretty rice

This makes a scrumptious side dish when you omit the meat, and an impressive appetizer if you choose to include it.

Ingredients

instant long grain rice
chili sauce
chopped green peppers, celery and/or onion
cooked meat chunks of any kind — chicken, ham, beef, etc.
  (use your leftovers)

Method

Prepare the rice according to package directions, using 1/2 the usual water and 1/2 chili sauce. Add the chopped ingredients as you do this.

Potato pudding muffins

Ingredients

1 large package instant potato pancakes
1 teaspoon (5 mL) baking powder

Method

Prepare according to package directions adding baking powder, and spoon the mixture into individual greased muffin tins. Bake at 350°F (180°C) until nicely browned (about 20 to 30 minutes). These make a great alternative to the usual potato dishes.

POTATO PUFFS PANACHE

You may use either plain potatoes or sweet potatoes for this recipe.

Ingredients

3 lbs. (1.5 kg) potatoes (sufficient for 8 people)
1/3 cup (75 mL) butter
Corn Flakes
grated Cheddar cheese

Method

Boil the potatoes until they are soft when pierced with a fork. (Peel before or after boiling). Meanwhile, mix the Corn Flakes with some grated Cheddar cheese — just enough of the latter to give the potatoes zing. When the potatoes are cooked, cool and mash with the butter. Form into balls and roll in the Corn Flake mixture. Bake on a shallow cookie sheet or pan, which has been well greased, at 350°F (180°C) for 15 to 20 minutes, or until crisp and brown.

SWEET POTATO PIE

Ingredients

2 cans sweet potatoes or yams with liquid
1/2 cup (100 mL) brown sugar
1 package colored miniature marshmallows
1 rounded tablespoon (15 mL) butter

Method

Drain the potatoes, saving 1/2 cup (100 ml) of the liquid from the cans. Mash the potatoes and butter into a buttered baking dish after mixing them with the liquid and brown sugar. Cover with marshmallows and bake, covered, at 350°F (180°C) for 20 minutes, then uncovered until the marshmallows begin to brown (about another 1/4 hour).

That'll do it casserole

So called because after wracking your brain thinking of a colorful, healthy elegant *and* easy dish that will be just right to accompany that smashing entrée you have selected so carefully, you come across this and exclaim: "That'll do it!"

Ingredients

1 bunch fresh broccoli
1 head cauliflower
3 or 4 slices Mozzarella and Cheddar cheese, torn into strips
butter
dash salt and pepper

Method

Cut the broccoli and cauliflower into small pieces and parboil (i.e., boil for about 4 minutes). In a buttered casserole dish, alternate layers of vegetables with strips of cheese, and dot each vegetable layer with butter and a dash of salt and pepper. Top with Cheddar cheese for color, and bake 1/2 hour.

Steaming Zucchini Casserole

Here's a beautiful way to introduce your family or friends to this often ignored friendly vegie.

Ingredients

1 lb. (500 g) zucchini
1   14 oz. (400 mL) can stewed tomatoes, drained
1 small can corn, drained
1 small can sliced mushrooms, drained
2 to 3 tablespoons (25 mL to 45 mL) margarine
3 tablespoons grated Parmesan cheese
2 tablespoons (25 mL) bread crumbs

Method

Wash the zucchini and slice into a buttered baking dish. Add the tomatoes, corn and mushrooms. Soften the margarine with the cheese and bread crumbs, and sprinkle over top. Bake at 350°F (180°C) for about 50 minutes, or until the zucchini is soft.

Broccoli almondine

Who'd want to plod through life without occasionally adding a splash of the unexpected to the ordinary? Why not uninhibit your broccoli? Take it from the simple to the sophisticated with just a little imagination.

Ingredients

2 10 oz. (300 g) packages frozen broccoli
1/4 cup (50 mL) butter or margarine
1/2 cup (100 mL) slivered almonds

Method

Cook the broccoli according to package directions. Drain, and put in an attractive serving dish. Melt the butter (or margarine) and add the nuts, cooking them gently until they are crisp and golden. Pour over the hot broccoli and serve.

Judy's favorite broccoli soufflé

Judy is a stylish young woman with a flair for elegant but easy entertaining. Her Favorite Broccoli Soufflé does double-duty as either a side dish or a light luncheon entrée, and if it's her pet recipe, it's got to be sensational.

Ingredients

2 10 oz. (300 g) packages frozen chopped broccoli, defrosted
3 eggs
6 tablespoons (85 mL) soft butter
2 tablespoons (25 mL) flour
1/2 cup (100 mL) frozen chopped onions, defrosted
1 8 oz. (250 g) jar Cheez Whiz
Ritz crackers

Method

Put the drained broccoli in a large bowl. Beat the eggs and pour over the broccoli. Then add all the other ingredients (except the crackers), and mix well together. Pour into a 2 quart (2L) soufflé dish (which has been lightly greased with a non-stick spray) and crush the Ritz crackers to spread on top. Bake at 325°F (160°C) for 1 hour and serve whenever the occasion demands something fabulous.

If served as an entrée, a simple lettuce salad completes the meal.

Cauliflower au Gratin

Ingredients

1 head cauliflower broken into florets
1/2 bottle Roquefort salad dressing, or bottled cheese spread
1/2 cup (125 mL) commercial sour cream
dried parsley (optional)

Method

There's no real reason why you have to stick with cauliflower for this side dish. Broccoli, zucchini or asparagus works just as well. It's your choice. Simply cook the vegetable in 1 inch (2.5 cm) of water, covered, for 5 to 6 minutes. Meanwhile, combine the dressing and sour cream and stir over a low heat. Then pour this mixture over the drained vegetable and serve. A sprinkling of dried parsley makes it even partier.

JEANNETTE'S TASTY baked ASPARAGUS

For the beginner or the expert, here's a dream of a side dish that spells success.

Ingredients

1 container bread crumbs
margarine
3 10 oz. (300 mL) cans cream of mushroom soup
8 eggs, hard-boiled and sliced
3 cans asparagus

Method

Grease a baking dish generously, and spread a layer of bread crumbs on the bottom. Dot with margarine, and cover with 1 can of the soup. Then layer with eggs, asparagus, soup, and so on, finishing with a sprinkle of bread crumbs. Bake at 350°F (180°C) for 3/4 hour.

GORGEOUS GREEN BEANS

(makes a lot — a perfect buffet dish)

Ingredients

2 packages frozen French-style green beans
1   10 oz. (300 mL) can mushroom soup
1/2 can milk
1/2 cup (100 mL) slivered almonds
1 can fried onion rings

Method

Soak the beans in salted water to defrost, then drain. Mix with soup and milk and put in a baking dish. Add the almonds and cover with the onions. Bake at 350°F (180°C) until hot and bubbly (about 20 minutes).

Half-baked beans

Nearly every recipe book boasts a marvelous method for preparing homemade baked beans. It's standard: you soak them, you bake them, you doctor them, and everyone's supposed to be thrilled. Frankly, I find it difficult to get bubbled over beans, so I've come up with a half-baked idea of my own. And it's not half-bad either!

Ingredients

1 can baked beans (not drained)
2 or 3 tablespoons (25 mL to 45 mL) brown sugar to taste
1 teaspoon (5 mL) hot dry mustard

Method

Mix all the ingredients together in a pot. Heat and serve.

HANGOVER PEARS

Ingredients

1 or 2 cans Bartlett pears, well drained
Grand Marnier liqueur — 3 to 4 oz. (100 mL)

Method

Put the pears in a bowl and cover them lightly with the Grand Marnier, filling the hollow spot in each pear. Refrigerate for several hours at least, or overnight. Serve as a dessert, of course, but better yet, use as a side dish with a heavy meat meal. When served right alongside a roast or bird, Hangover Pears are a gorgeous garnish.

Avocado dream appetizer

Avocados make scrumptious salads, and terrible trees. The only nice thing about the pit, if you ask me, is that when you remove it, you are left with a perfectly sculpted hole to stuff with something savory.

Ingredients

2 ripe avocados (sufficient for 4 people)
2 small tins small or medium shrimps, crab or lobster meat, well drained
1/2 cup (100 mL) thick French or Thousand Island salad dressing
parsley sprigs (optional)
cherry tomatoes (optional)

Method

Split the avocados with a knife and discard the pits. Mix the seafood and dressing together and mound a portion into each cavity. Serve individually on a fresh green bed of lettuce and garnish with parsley sprigs and cherry tomatoes.

Stuffed avocado à la joanne

This tasty variation of the Avocado Dream Appetizer (see p. 116) is another quick and easy recipe using that most refined of fruits along with crab meat.

Ingredients

2 ripe avocados (sufficient for 4 people)
1 package frozen crab meat, defrosted
1 small onion, chopped
1 small jar Kraft sandwich spread
lemon juice

Method

Drain and mix the crab meat with the onion to taste. Scoop the avocado out of its skin, in bite-sized chunks. Put a little lemon juice on the empty skin to keep it from turning color. Combine the crab and avocado together and then add enough sandwich spread to make a creamy combination. Put this mixture back into the skins.

Clever crab meat judith

It's clever because it knows how to fit in anywhere — as an hors d'oeuvre, appetizer or entrée.

Ingredients

1 10 oz. (300 mL) can cream of shrimp soup
1/4 cup (50 mL) of sherry combined with 1/4 cup (50 mL) milk
1/4 cup (50 mL) grated Cheddar cheese
1 package frozen green peas
1 lb. (500 g) frozen crab meat, defrosted
1/2 lb. (250 g) frozen cooked shrimp, defrosted

Method

In a medium-sized pot, combine the soup, milk and sherry, and cheese. Then add the peas, crab meat and shrimp. Heat thoroughly until it starts to bubble. Simmer a few more minutes.

Serve this delicate mixture on patty shells for individual starters, or on wild rice for a main luncheon dish. Using a little less liquid, it will sit prettily in tiny tart shells as a hot hors d'oeuvre.

Seafood Appetizer

Ingredients

1 large or 2 small tins crab or lobster meat, or small shrimps, well
   drained
1 10 oz. (300 mL) can mushroom soup
1/2 cup (125 mL) peas

Method

Combine the seafood, soup and peas. If you want to serve this on
patty shells, simmer the ingredients until they are hot and then
pour over the shells. But, if you want to go all out with large sea
shells (you can find these in most gourmet food shops), fill each of
them and bake on a cookie sheet in the oven at 350°F (180°C)
until they bubble (about 20 minutes).

Seafood party spread

Ingredients

1 8 oz. (250 g) tin crab or lobster meat, well drained
3/4 cup (175 mL) French salad dressing
1 tablespoon (15 mL) relish

Method

Combine all the ingredients. Serve in a pretty bowl encircled by crackers or toast rounds, or pour into little puff pastry shells for individual appetizers.

Helene's heavenly mock crab spread

Ingredients

1 box frozen cod fish filets, boned and separated
1 bay leaf
sprinkling onion flakes
dash salt and pepper
shot Tabasco
ketchup to taste
mayonnaise to taste

Method

Poach the fish in a frying pan in 1 inch (2.5 cm) of water. Include the bay leaf, onion flakes and salt and pepper in this process. When the fish is tender, drain it. Discard the bay leaf. Mash the fish and refrigerate overnight in a covered container. Then, whenever you're ready, add a little ketchup and the Tabasco and mayonnaise. Serve with crackers.

Funky fruit dip

Ingredients

1 cup (250 mL) commercial sour cream
1/4 cup (50 mL) brown sugar
bowl of fresh strawberries or selection of fresh fruit, cut into chunks

Method

Mix the sour cream and brown sugar together. Serve alongside the fruit which has been stabbed with colorful toothpicks. It's a surprisingly delightful flavor combination.

Party Fruit Dip

Ingredients

30 to 40 miniature marshmallows
1 pint (500 mL) commercial sour cream
fresh fruit cut into chunks, or canned peaches or apricots

Method

Mix the marshmallows with the sour cream and refrigerate overnight. Serve surrounded by the fruit chunks for dipping, or use the dip to top peaches or apricots for a simple but savory dessert.

Vegetable party dips

Make these up in four attractive servers and surround with a beautiful arrangement of raw vegetables, such as cauliflower, mushrooms, carrots, celery, green peppers, cucumbers and broccoli florets. By the way, the dressings in a jar seem to work better than the dressings in a bottle.

Dip 1
2 cups (500 mL) French salad dressing mixed with 1/2 cup (125 mL) commercial sour cream

Dip 2
2 cups (500 mL) Roquefort salad dressing mixed with 1/2 cup (125 mL) commercial sour cream

Dip 3
1 packet dehydrated onion soup mixed with commercial sour cream to taste. (Adding 1 tin crab meat and a dash of Worcestershire makes a nice variation.)

Dip 4
avocado salad dressing

ỉVER CANAPÉ

Ingredients

1 package frozen pie crust dough, defrosted
1 lb (500 g) tub chopped liver (from a deli)

Method

Roll the crust out thinly and fill with the tub of liver making a sausage shape. (Save extra dough for more rolls.) Roll up and mark the dough with mini slashes about 1-1/2 inches (4 cm) apart. Bake on a lightly sprayed cookie sheet at 425°F (220°C) until golden brown (read package directions for exact time). Slice and serve immediately. In other words, pop these into the oven when the doorbell rings.

Dogs in a blanket

Ingredients

party-sized wieners (the tiny ones)
1 or 2 packages crescent dinner rolls (the easy-bake kind which
you'll find in your grocer's cooler)

Method

Roll the wieners in the dough and bake on a lightly sprayed cookie
sheet at 350°F (180°C) until golden brown (about 1/4 hour).

MARINATED MUSHROOMS

Ingredients

1 can whole mushrooms
1/2 bottle Italian salad dressing

Method

Put the drained mushrooms in a small saucepan and cover with the dressing. Bring to a boil, then chill for at least several hours. Drain the mushrooms again before serving, and decorate with fancy toothpicks, or serve as a side dish at the table.

Startled stuffed celery

Ingredients

1 container small curd cottage cheese
1/2 cup (100 mL) salad dressing of any kind (a spicy one is
   best)
2 drops Worcestershire sauce
celery

Method

Blend all the ingredients and fill the celery cavities for a startling
taste tempter.

Desserts Deluxe

At least once a day, nearly every day, you have the opportunity to be terrific. At least once a party, surely every party, you have the chance to be absolutely dynamite! The challenge to rise to such heights occurs so often that it would be madness to neglect it, for, happily, dessert comes at the end of every meal. While the rest of the meal may be a spectacular (and instant) success, dessert can be your crowning achievement. It's the time to let your imagination run wild; to go mad with garnish; to go crazy with color — in short, to go fabulous with dessert.

Although we probably hate to admit it in this age of body consciousness, many of us would gladly give up our vitaminized staples for a hunk of something savory; for a heap of mouthwatering lusciousness; for that *pièce de résistance* — a delicious dessert — which surely must be the password to gracious entertaining.

As a matter of fact, many of the most successful parties actually exclude main courses! Dessert luncheons have proven a most desirable way to entertain easily and well. Spread your table with a collection of wonderful yummies and you needn't concern yourself further. It certainly takes the quandary out of meal planning. Triumphant evening parties, too, are often centered around a tantalizing sweet table. Let your guests choose from a fascinating variety of delectable desserts and forget all about mere mortal fare.

131

In the following dessert section, you will find an array of easy but impressive creations. Prepare them according to directions, or use your imagination to invent original variations on the theme. And do remember to garnish lavishly. Chocolate swirls (made with a simple carrot peeler against a piece of semi-sweet chocolate), almond slivers, chocolate chips, maraschino cherries, coconut bits — almost anything sweet and pretty may be added as a last touch that says you have flair.

Heater's cherry cheese cake

Ingredients

18 Graham wafers, crushed
1/4 lb. (125 g) melted butter
1/4 cup (50 mL) sugar
1 package Dream Whip
1 large (8 oz. — 200 g) package Philadelphia cream cheese
1 can cherry pie filling

Method

Mix the wafers, sugar and butter and pat into a lightly sprayed spring form baking pan. Bake for 10 minutes at 350°F (180°C). Meanwhile, whip the Dream Whip and mix it with the cream cheese (using an electric beater at medium speed) until the two ingredients are well combined. Remove the spring form from the oven, cool, and fill with the creamed mixture. Chill. When firm, top with cherry pie filling and remove the sides of the spring form before serving.

Penny's cherries jubilee

Ingredients

1 14 oz. (400 mL) can pitted Bing cherries
1/3 cup (75 mL) red currant jelly
1/4 cup (50 mL) brandy
vanilla ice cream

Method

Melt the jelly in a skillet on medium heat, stirring often. To the melted jelly add the drained cherries, stirring occasionally to coat the cherries. Pour the brandy into the middle of the mixture and heat undisturbed for 2 to 3 minutes. Light the brandy, and while it's flaming, pour it over the vanilla ice cream which you have put into attractive glasses.

Appropriately, you would do all this over a small flame at the dining table. But if you haven't a showy skillet, don't dismay; the taste is so disarmingly good, your guests will never notice they missed the theatrics.

BANANA CREAM PIE

Ingredients

1 frozen pie crust shell
2 or 3 bananas, sliced
1 4 oz. (100 g) package instant vanilla or banana pudding
1/2 pint (250 mL) whipping cream, or frozen whipped topping

Method

Bake the crust according to package directions and cool. Place the bananas on the crust and cover with the pudding (which you have made, again according to package directions). Chill until firm. Top with the whipped cream.

Deep dish peach or apple crisp

Ingredients

1 large can apple or peach pie filling
1 cup (250 mL) flour
1/2 cup (100 mL) melted butter
1 cup (250 mL) brown sugar
ice cream or table cream (optional)

Method

Divide the pie filling into lightly sprayed, individual Pyrex dishes.
Mix the flour, butter and sugar, rubbing together with your hands,
and top each dish with this mixture. Bake at 350°F (180°C) for 30
to 35 minutes. Serve with table cream or a scoop of ice cream.

Classic strudel

Ingredients

1 box frozen strudel dough, thawed
2 10 oz (300 mL) jars pineapple marmalade or strawberry jam
1 package desiccated coconut
1 3 oz. (100 g) package chopped walnuts
1 small bag golden raisins

Method

Spread 3 or 4 leaves of dough from the box onto a slightly
dampened cloth. Cover the dough all over with the marmalade or
jam. Sprinkle generously with the coconut, walnuts and raisins.
Roll up the dough, tuck the ends under, and bake at 350°F
(180°C) for about 20 to 30 minutes on a lightly sprayed cookie
sheet. Slice as much as you need for your guests and freeze the rest
for the next time.

Tid bit dessert

Ingredients

1 20 oz. (600 mL) can crushed pineapple, well drained
1 11 oz. (300 mL) can mandarin oranges, well drained
1 cup (250 mL) miniature marshmallows
1 medium can fruit cocktail
1/2 teaspoon (2 mL) salt
4 oz. (100 g) desiccated coconut
1/2 cup (100 mL) maraschino cherries
2 cups (500 mL) commercial sour cream

Method

Mix the whole batch together and serve chilled in champagne glasses.

Ambrosia

Ingredients

1 large package strawberry Jello
1 14 oz. (400 mL) can fruit cup, drained
3 bananas, sliced
1 cup (250 mL) miniature marshmallows
1-1/2 pints (850 mL) whipping cream
1 jelly roll (or 4 small ones)
desiccated coconut and almonds or walnuts (optional)
maraschino cherries

Method

Make the Jello according to package directions and allow to set.
When firm, whip for 1 minute using an electric beater at low speed.
Then add the fruit cup, bananas, marshmallows (and coconut and
nuts if you wish) and stir. Whip the cream and fold into previous
mixture. Line a pretty bowl with a layer of sliced jelly roll (this is
particularly effective in an oversized brandy snifter) and spoon in
enough of the mixture to keep the jelly roll in place. Add another
row and spoon in the remaining mixture. Garnish with maraschino
cherries.

Jack's gin jello

This dessert is bound to liven up the after-dinner conversation. But then again, if you make it in a mold and serve it as a side dish along with your meal, it might get the party rolling a whole lot sooner.

Ingredients

1 package lemon or lime Jello
gin
maraschino cherries

Method

Prepare the Jello in the usual manner, substituting gin for 1/2 the water. Pour into champagne glasses and when firm, dot each serving with a maraschino cherry.

Party balls

Makes 5-6 dozen

Ingredients

1 10 oz. (300 g) package dried apricots
3/4 cup (175 mL) corn syrup
1-1/2 cups (350 mL) chopped nuts (pecans are especially
  good)
2-1/2 cups (600 mL) desiccated coconut
1/2 cup (100 mL) sugar

Method

Cut the apricots into small pieces. Place them in a saucepan and
add the syrup. Cook over medium heat until the consistency of
applesauce is reached. Then stir in the nuts and coconut, and cool.
Form into small balls and roll in sugar.

Razzle dazzle rice krispies

This, the ultimate in instant recipes, lets you razzle dazzle your kids or your company.

Ingredients

1 super-sized milk chocolate bar, melted
1/3 box Rice Krispies

Method

To the melted chocolate, add the Rice Krispies. Drop with a spoon onto waxed paper and allow to harden.

Nutty ice cream pie

Ingredients

2 large packages lime Jello
1 pint (500 mL) butter pecan ice cream
1 large can crushed pineapple (with juice)
fresh mint leaves

Method

Dissolve the Jello using only the hot water called for on the package. To this, add the softened ice cream and whip for 2 or 3 minutes using an electric mixer at medium speed. Add the pineapple and juice, and pour into a ring mold. Serve on a glistening silver platter garnished with mint leaves.

CE CREAM GOURMET

Ingredients

1 quart (1 L) vanilla ice cream
4 or 5 Crispy Crunch chocolate bars
3 inch (8 cm) square of halvah
1 jar chocolate sauce (optional)

Method

Pat softened ice cream into a spring form baking pan, and top with crushed chocolate bars and crushed halvah. Refreeze. Remove the sides of the spring form to serve. If you wish, heat the chocolate sauce and spoon over individual slices when serving.

Sherbet crème de menthe

Ingredients

1/3 cup (75 mL) crème de menthe liqueur
3 pints (2 L) lime sherbet
maraschino cherries
fresh mint leaves

Method

Mix the softened sherbet with the crème de menthe and press into
a spring form baking pan, or into individual molds. Refreeze.
Unmold to serve and trim lavishly with cherries and mint leaves.

Crackin' ice cream cake

Ingredients

1 quart (1 L) vanilla ice cream
1/2 lb. (250 g) peanut brittle, crushed
1 package chocolate wafers
1 bottle butterscotch syrup

Method

Soften the ice cream and mix with the crushed peanut brittle. Line a spring form pan with the chocolate wafers, and press the ice cream mixture into it. Freeze. When ready to serve, heat the butterscotch syrup and place in a gravy boat with a ladle to pour over each slice. And remember to remove the sides of the spring form!

Chocolate orange ice box cake

Ingredients

1 package chocolate wafers
3 tablespoons (45 mL) melted butter
1 large package orange Jello
2 cups (500 mL) hot water
1 quart (1 L) vanilla ice cream
1 11 oz. (300 mL) can mandarin oranges

Method

Grease a spring form baking pan. Crush most of the wafers, mix crumbs (saving some) with butter and press into the bottom of the spring form. Place the remaining uncrushed wafers around the sides. Now, mix the water and Jello, and cut in the ice cream. Whip these three ingredients together and pour half into the cake pan. Arrange half of the orange slices on top of this and pour in the rest of the Jello/water/ice cream mixture. Top with the remaining orange slices and chocolate wafer crumbs. Chill for several hours and serve, after removing the sides of the spring form.

Chocolate log

Ingredients

1 package chocolate wafers
1 pint (500 mL) whipping cream (do *not* use aerosol type here)
1 square semi-sweet chocolate

Method

Whip the cream stiffly. Generously spread both sides of a wafer
with the whipping cream and stick another wafer to it. Standing
these two wafers on their sides, add more whipping cream to the
clean side of each wafer and continue on in this manner until you
have a log about 8 to 10 inches (20 cm to 25 cm) in length. Make a
second log and attach it alongside the first using extra cream, if
necessary, to make the two logs adhere to each other. Spread the
remaining cream over the entire log and garnish with chocolate
swirls (made by stroking the semi-sweet chocolate square with a
carrot peeler). Chill for several hours at least. When serving, slice
on an angle.

Chocolate cookie crinkles

Ingredients

5 to 6 squares semi-sweet chocolate
3 to 4 oz (100 g) peanuts, cut in half
3 to 4 oz. (100 g) dry chow mein noodles

Method

Melt the chocolate in a pot on the stove over medium heat.
Remove from the stove. Add the other ingredients, mixing well, to
cover with the chocolate. Drop by the spoonful onto waxed paper.
Let harden.

Chocolate pudding pie

Ingredients

8 Graham wafers (or packaged Graham wafer crumbs)
1/8 lb. (50 mL) melted butter
2 4 oz. (100 g) packages instant chocolate pudding
1/2 to 1 pint (250 mL to 500 mL) whipping cream, whipped
1 square semi-sweet chocolate

Method

Crumb the wafers and add butter (or, if using the packaged crumbs, prepare according to package directions — without adding the sugar) and pat into a pie plate. Fill with the pudding which you have made, again according to package instructions, and chill for several hours (or until firm). Top with whipped cream and garnish with chocolate swirls (made by stroking the semi-sweet chocolate square with a carrot peeler).

Graham wafer almond fingers

Here's a dainty pick-up to add a touch of pretty to any sweet table.

Ingredients

1/3 to 1/2 lb. (150 g to 250 g) butter
1 cup (250 mL) brown sugar
1 to 2 squares semi-sweet chocolate (optional)
24 Graham wafers
1-1/2 packages sliced almonds

Method

Combine the butter and sugar on the stove (add the chocolate, if desired). Cook until a drop of the mixture in cold water forms a soft ball. Pour this hot liquid over the Graham wafers which have been laid out on a lightly sprayed cookie sheet. Sprinkle with nuts. Bake at 350°F (180°C) for 7 to 8 minutes. Cut into fingers while still hot.

Napoleons

Ingredients

Graham wafers
2 large packages vanilla pudding and pie filling
1 pint (500 mL) whipped cream or prepared whipped topping
2 egg whites
1-1/2 cups (350 mL) icing sugar
chocolate syrup

Method

Line the bottom of an oven-to-table pan with Graham wafers, and
cover with the vanilla pudding, which you have made according to
package instructions. (If it's the cooked type, let it cool.) Add
another layer of Graham wafers and top with whipping cream.
Then add the last layer of wafers. Beat the egg whites, gradually
adding the icing sugar, and spread over the top. Drizzle the
chocolate syrup over it all and refrigerate for a day.

ynne's favorite sour cream coffee cake

Ingredients

Cake
1 Duncan Hines yellow or lemon cake mix
1 4 oz. (100 g) package instant vanilla pudding
4 eggs
1/2 cup (100 mL) vegetable oil
1 8 or 10 oz. (250 mL or 300 mL) carton commercial
  sour cream

Topping
1/2 cup (100 mL) brown sugar
2 tablespoons (25 mL) cinnamon
2 tablespoons (25 mL) unsweetened cocoa
4 teaspoons (20 mL) white sugar
2 2 oz. (50 g) packages ground nuts

Method

Combine all the topping ingredients and set aside. Beat all the cake
ingredients with an electric mixer at medium speed for 2 minutes.
Grease or spray a tube pan, and spread some of the topping
mixture on the bottom. Now, alternate cake mix and topping,
ending with cake mix. Bake at 350°F (180°C) for 50 to 60
minutes. Check to see if baking is done with a toothpick, which
should come out clean when poked into the cake.

153

Pineapple party cake

Ingredients

1 sponge cake (buy it ready-made)
1 small can crushed pineapple, drained
1/2 pint (250 mL) whipping cream

Method

Divide the cake into 2 layers. Whip the cream and then fold in the pineapple. Spread this mixture between the layers and on top of the cake. Serve on a pretty silver or glass tray.

Sponge cake jubilee

Ingredients

1 sponge cake (buy it ready-made)
2 14 oz. (400 mL) cans pitted Bing cherries
1 can whole cranberries, with juice
1 teaspoon (5 mL) flour
1/2 cup (125 mL) sweet sherry

Method

Heat the cherries and cranberries, adding flour very gradually to thicken. When the mixture comes to a boil, add the sherry and remove from the heat. Pour this scarlet sauce over cake slices at the table.

Special sponge cake surprise

Ingredients

1 sponge cake (buy it ready-made)
3 Oh Henry! chocolate bars
1 pint (500 mL) whipping cream, whipped

Method

Crush the chocolate bars and mix with the whipped cream. Cut cake into 3 layers horizontally and spread the middle section with the cream mixture, reserving slightly more than half to cover the top and sides.

Rich lemon cake

Ingredients

1 lemon cake mix
4 eggs
1/2 cup (100 mL) oil
1 cup (250 mL) commercial sour cream
1 4 oz. (100 g) package instant lemon pudding

Method

Beat everything together for 10 minutes, using an electric beater at medium speed. Put in a greased tube pan and bake for 1 hour at 325°F (160°C). To see if baking is done, poke the cake with a toothpick, which should come out clean.

Chocolate spice cake

Ingredients

1 spice cake mix
4 eggs
1/2 cup (100 mL) oil
1 cup (250 mL) commercial sour cream
1 4 oz. (100 g) package instant chocolate pudding
1/2 cup (125 mL) chocolate chips
2 chocolate bars (dark or milk chocolate, with or without nuts)

Method

Beat everything (except the chocolate chips and chocolate bars) for 10 minutes, using an electric beater at medium speed. Stir in the chocolate chips and pour the entire mixture into a greased tube pan. Bake at 325°F (160°C) for 1 hour. Test to see if done with a toothpick. Cool, then glaze by melting the chocolate bars and drizzling over the top of the cake.

TANGY APRICOT CAKE

Ingredients

Cake
1 lemon cake mix
1 4 oz. (100 g) package lemon pudding and pie filling
4 eggs
3/4 cup (175 mL) oil
3/4 cup (175 mL) apricot nectar
1 or 2 drops lemon extract

Glaze
1 cup (250 mL) sugar
1/3 cup (75 mL) apricot nectar
dash apricot brandy (optional)

Method

Mix all the cake ingredients together, using an electric beater at medium speed for 5 minutes. Bake 1 hour in a greased and lightly floured tube pan at 325°F (160°C). Test to see if done with a toothpick. Cool for 1 hour. Boil the glaze ingredients for 5 minutes. Let cool for another 5 minutes and then drizzle over the cake.

Fantastic banana flan, or strawberry sure cake

To make this really exciting, you should treat yourself to a proper flan pan — the kind that allows you to separate the bottom from the nicely fluted sides. Failing that, an ordinary large pie plate will do; or if you're really frantically rushed, you may simply buy the ready-prepared flan base, flat-type cake which is found in any large grocery store.

Ingredients

Shortbread Base
1 lb. (500 g) butter
1 cup (250 mL) flour
1/2 cup (100 mL) sugar

Filling
4 medium bananas, or 1 pint (250 mL) strawberries
1 4 oz. (100 g) package instant vanilla pudding
1 package Dream Whip

Method

The shortbread base needn't cause you to panic. There's no rolling out to do here. To make the dough, just cream the butter and add the flour and sugar, mixing with an electric beater at medium speed. Then, firmly press the dough into the flan pan to form a layer about 1/4 inch (0.5 cm) thick. Depending on the size of your pan, you will likely find you have a handful of dough left over. No problem, it also makes terrific cookies! When the dough is pressed down well, prick it generously with a fork and pop it into a 350°F (180°C) oven for about 20 minutes, or until it's golden brown. Remove from the oven and cool. Then slice up the bananas or strawberries and spread them over the base. Mix up the pudding according to package instructions and spoon it over the fruit. When set (refrigerating for a few minutes helps speed up the process), whip up the Dream Whip topping following package directions and spread on top. Don't remove the sides of the pan until you're ready to serve. And when you do serve, you'll discover the most marvelous marriage of fruit, cream and pastry ever!

Jill's flantastic

In a moment of sheer inspiration, Jill came up with this flantastic dessert which looks professionally smashing and takes only mini-minutes to build.

Ingredients

1 cake flan base (buy it ready-made)
2 4 oz. (100 mL) tins vanilla dessert, or 1 4 oz. (100 g) package
   instant vanilla pudding
whatever fresh fruit or combination of fruits you wish (e.g.
   strawberries, green seedless grapes, peach slices, apple
   slices)
1 10 oz. (300 mL) jar apple jelly

Method

Cover the cake base with a layer of pudding. Begin in the center of the flan and arrange the fruit in pleasing circles, covering the entire base except for the outside lip. Now, melt the apple jelly and spoon it on top using as much as you need to glaze the entire flantastic.

Apricot Mountain

I have to confess that this recipe involves a bit of tedium as far as preparing the meringues is concerned. If you can buy them ready-made (and they are available at most good European bakeries) so much the better. If not, don't be intimidated. Meringues are really quite easy to make, though I admit they are inclined to be fiddly. But Apricot Mountain will surely be one of your claims to culinary fame and well worth the extra effort.

Ingredients

Meringues
6 large egg whites
1/8 teaspoon (pinch) salt
1 teaspoon (5 mL) white vinegar
1/2 teaspoon (2 mL) vanilla extract
2 cups (500 mL) sugar

Mountain
1 medium can apricots
2 11 oz. cans mandarin oranges
1 package long shredded coconut
1 8 oz. (250 g) package slivered almonds
4 packages Dream Whip

Method

To make the meringues, beat the egg whites, salt, vinegar and vanilla with an electric beater at high speed until fluffy. Then add the sugar slowly while continuing to beat until the mixture is stiff and shiny. Cover a large cookie sheet with brown paper (a torn paper bag will do) and drop the mixture onto the paper to make 18 cookies. Bake at 275°F (140°C) for 3/4 hour, then at 250°F (120°C) for another 1/2 to 3/4 hour. Remove from the oven and immediately peel off the paper. Store the meringues in a plastic bag when cool. They will keep until you are ready to make your mountain.

From here to the finish line, it's a cinch. Just drain the fruit and put it aside for the moment. Toast the coconut and almonds in the oven at 325°F (160°C). Meanwhile, whip up the 4 packages of Dream Whip according to package directions. Now, pile it all together in the following manner:

On a large cake plate or silver tray, place the first layer of seven meringues (six in a circle, one in the center). Spread on some Dream Whip and sprinkle with half the fruit and some coconut and almonds. Form the second layer of six meringues the same way, using up the remaining fruit, but leaving some coconut and almonds for garnish. The last layer of five meringues should be covered with Dream Whip and sprinkled liberally with coconut. Stab the mountain all over with the remaining slivered almonds. Stand back and admire. Then serve.

Appendix

Some Metric Units

Unit (Symbol)	Replaces
centimetre (cm)	inch, foot
metre (m)	foot, yard
degree Celsius (°C)	degree Fahrenheit
millilitre (mL)	teaspoon, tablespoon, cup, fluid ounce, pint
litre (L)	pint, quart, gallon
gram (g)	ounce (avoirdupois), pound
kilogram (kg)	pound

Metric Relationships

$$100 \text{ cm} = 1 \text{ m}$$
$$1000 \text{ mL} = 1 \text{ L}$$
$$1000 \text{ g} = 1 \text{ kg}$$

The first step to take in the metric kitchen is to acquire some metric measures. Don't, for heaven's sake, try to use imperial measures for metric recipes, or vice versa. Sets of metric spoons and dry measures come in both plastic (cheap) and stainless steel (not so cheap, but more durable). Liquid measures are available in Pyrex, as always. (The 500 mL size is the most useful, unless you usually cook for one or throw a lot of parties.)

Here are the sizes to look for; they're used in all metric recipes:

Standard Metric Kitchen Measures

Small Measures (Spoons)
  1 mL
  2 mL
  5 mL (about 1 teaspoon)
15 mL (about 1 tablespoon)
25 mL (coffee measure)

Dry Measures
  50 mL
125 mL
250 mL (about 1 cup)

Liquid Measures
  250 mL, graduated every 25 mL (about 1 cup)
  500 mL, graduated every 50 mL (about 1 pint)
1000 mL, graduated every 50 mL and 100 mL (about 1 quart)

If you're hoarding a box of tried-and-true, family-tradition, old-standby recipes that you want to change to metric measures, here's how I did it for this book. Follow the same method and you won't go far wrong:

Match the ingredients given in your recipe with the metric measurements in the charts below. (I've included the actual conversions so you can get a feel for the quantity changes.) Generally, it's a good idea to match increases or decreases in "wet" and "dry" ingredients, but most recipes allow a hefty margin of error.

Where a choice of measures is given in the chart, use either what's available or the amount reflecting your taste for that ingredient.

And remember, simplicity is always better. That's why I have changed 1 cup to 250 mL (not 227 mL) and 325°F to 160°C (not 163°C).

Customary-to-Metric Conversions Used in this Book

Temperatures

Fahrenheit	Celsius	(Actual Conversion)
100°F	40°C	(38°C)
125°F	50°C	(52°C)
150°F	65°C	(66°C)
175°F	80°C	(79°C)
200°F	90°C	(93°C)
225°F	110°C	(107°C)
250°F	120°C	(121°C)
275°F	140°C	(135°C)
300°F	150°C	(148°C)
325°F	160°C	(163°C)
350°F	180°C	(177°C)
375°F	190°C	(191°C)
400°F	200°C	(204°C)
425°F	220°C	(218°C)
450°F	230°C	(232°C)

Cooking Times

By the Pound	By the Kilogram	(Actual Conversion)
20 min/lb.	45 min/kg	(44 min/kg)
25 min/lb.	55 min/kg	(55 min/kg)
30 min/lb.	65 min/kg	(66 min/kg)

Small (Spoon) Measurements

Customary Size	Metric Size	(Actual Conversion)
1/8 teaspoon	pinch	(0.6 mL)
1/4 teaspoon	1 mL*	(1.2 mL)
1/2 teaspoon	2 mL*	(2.4 mL)
1 teaspoon	5 mL*	(4.7 mL)
1-1/2 teaspoons	7 mL	(7.1 mL)
2 teaspoons	10 mL	(9.5 mL)
4 teaspoons	20 mL	(19.0 mL)
1 tablespoon	15 mL*	(14.2 mL)
1-1/2 tablespoons	20 mL	(21.3 mL)
2 tablespoons	{ 25 mL* / 30 mL	(28.4 mL)
3 tablespoons	45 mL	(42.6 mL)
4 tablespoons	{ 50 mL* / 60 mL	(56.8 mL)
5 tablespoons	75 mL	(71.0 mL)
6 tablespoons	85 mL	(85.2 mL)

* standard kitchen measure

Capacity Measurements

Customary Size	Metric Size	(Actual Conversion)
10 fl. oz.	300 mL	(284 mL)
11 fl. oz.	300 mL	(313 mL)
12 fl. oz.	350 mL	(341 mL)
14 fl. oz.	400 mL	(398 mL)
16 fl. oz.	450 mL	(455 mL)
18 fl. oz.	500 mL*	(511 mL)
20 fl. oz.	600 mL	(568 mL)
1/4 cup	50 mL*	(56.8 mL)
1/3 cup	75 mL	(75.8 mL)
1/2 cup	{ 100 mL / 125 mL*	(114 mL)
3/4 cup	175 mL	(170 mL)
1 cup	250 mL*	(227 mL)
1-1/4 cups	300 mL	(284 mL)
1-1/2 cups	350 mL	(340 mL)
1-3/4 cups	400 mL	(398 mL)
2 cups	450 mL	(455 mL)
2-1/2 cups	500 mL*	(568 mL)
3 cups	700 mL	(681 mL)

1/4 pint	{ 125 mL * { 150 mL	(142 mL)
1/2 pint	{ 250 mL * { 300 mL	(284 mL)
1 pint	500 mL *	(568 mL)
1-1/2 pints	850 mL	(852 mL)
2 pints	1 L *	(1.1 L)
3 pints	{ 1.5 L { 2 L	(1.7 L)
1 quart	1 L *	(1.1 L)
1-1/2 quarts	1.5 L	(1.7 L)
2 quarts	2 L	(2.3 L)

* standard kitchen measure

Mass (Weight) Measurements

Customary	Metric Size	(Actual Conversion)
2 oz.	50 g	(56.7 g)
3 oz.	85 g	(85.0 g)
4 oz.	100 g	(113 g)
5 oz.	150 g	(142 g)
6 oz.	175 g	(170 g)
7 oz.	200 g	(198 g)
8 oz.	{ 200 g / 250 g	(227 g)
9 oz.	250 g	(255 g)
10 oz.	300 g	(283 g)
12 oz.	350 g	(340 g)
14 oz.	400 g	(397 g)
1/8 lb.	50 g	(56.7 g)
1/4 lb.	{ 100 g / 125 g	(113 g)
1/3 lb.	150 g	(151 g)
1/2 lb.	250 g	(227 g)
3/4 lb.	350 g	(340 g)
1 lb.	{ 450 g / 500 g	(454 g)
1-1/4 lbs.	600 g	(567 g)
1-1/2 lbs.	700 g	(680 g)
1-3/4 lbs.	800 g	(794 g)

2 lbs.	1 kg	(0.9 kg)
2-1/2 lbs.	1 kg 1.25 kg	(1.1 kg)
3 lbs.	1.5 kg	(1.4 kg)
4 lbs.	2 kg	(1.8 kg)
5 lbs.	2.5 kg	(2.3 kg)

Linear Measurements

Inches	Centimetres	(Actual Conversion)
1/4 inch	0.5 cm	(0.6 cm)
1/2 inch	1 cm	(1.3 cm)
3/4 inch	2 cm	(1.9 cm)
1 inch	2.5 cm	(2.5 cm)
1-1/2 inches	4 cm	(3.8 cm)
2 inches	5 cm	(5.1 cm)
3 inches	8 cm	(7.6 cm)
4 inches	10 cm	(10.2 cm)